WILL MY CHILDREN
GO TO HEAVEN?

WILL MY CHILDREN GO TO HEAVEN?

*Hope and Help
for Believing Parents*

Edward N. Gross

P&R
P U B L I S H I N G
P.O. BOX 817 • PHILLIPSBURG • NEW JERSEY 08865-0817

Unless otherwise indicated, Scripture quotations are from the New American Standard Bible. Copyright by the Lockman Foundation 1960, 1962, 1963, 1968, 1971, 1973, 1975, 1977. Italics indicate emphasis added.

Printed in the United States of America

Library of Congress Cataloging-in-Publication Data

Gross, Edward N.
    Will my children go to heaven? : hope and help for believing parents / Edward N. Gross.
        p.   cm.
    Includes bibliographical references.
    ISBN 0-87552-246-7 (trade-paper)
    1. Children—Religious life. 2. Parents—Religious life. 3. Family—Religious life. 4. Parenting—Religious aspects—Christianity. 5. Discipline of children—Religious aspects—Christianity. I. Title.
    BV4571.G75 1995
    248.8'45—dc20   95-11834

Contents

Preface

Let me offer several important explanations and a clarification before you delve into this book. I will express them in a simple question-and-answer format. They come here, at the outset, in order to ensure that you understand both the subject of this book and its author. Please take time to read them carefully.

1. *Why are there so many personal illustrations?* Most good books are well illustrated. The sources of my illustrations are mainly two: the Bible and personal experience. I have chosen to use a lot of biblical examples because God included them in Scripture "for our instruction" (Rom. 15:4). It is His will for us to learn from the lives of people portrayed in the Bible. And I have used quite a few personal illustrations because I know that they are true. My wife and children have agreed to let me "open the curtain" so that you can look into our home. I will show you how we are trying to follow Christ in raising our children. Both successes and failures are shared so that we may all learn together.

Some people, upon hearing what I have been writing about, have said, "You surely are brave." I suspect that some have really meant, "Boy, are you stupid!" It is true that I am exposing myself and my family to unusual scrutiny and possible criticism. I do that not because I think we have all the answers or are doing everything right. Far from it. But these personal illustrations do show how earnestly and thoroughly we are *trying* to live as Christians in a very non-Christian culture. It is not easy to raise four children (ages 16, 14, 11, and 9) in a distinctively Christian way. Yet it is rewarding and can even be fun. I hope that by my showing you glimpses of my own family's life, you will be encouraged to trust God's grace for you and your family as well.

2. *What is the main point of this book?* I will show from Scripture that parents can be sure that their children will be saved and go to heaven. Their assurance is based on God's faithfulness to perform the promises He has made to believing parents and their families. It also grows from their determination to do their part as they depend on His grace. These promises of God, then, are conditional—parents do have an important part to play in their fulfillment. Yet every fulfillment of a divine promise is itself a product of God's grace. Since Jesus' righteousness is the foundation of all our success, our parental responsibilities can be fulfilled only in the spirit of faith. And so, children are not saved because of their parents; they are saved by grace through the redemption of Jesus Christ. Parents are simply the channel through which the message of this salvation is normally conveyed.

3. *Are there any exceptions to this principle?* If faithful parents are given a true promise of spiritual life for their children, then there can be no exceptions to that promise. If God has made such a promise to parents, and if any of their children perish even though the parents have fulfilled their part of the agreement, then we have a serious problem.

Does God keep His promises? All Christians believe that He does. The real issue, then, is this: Has God made such a promise to parents concerning the salvation of their children? After reading the early chapters of this book, in which I present my understanding of the biblical data, you will have to answer that question for yourself.

There is one urgent clarification that needs to be made. God usually fulfills His promise to parents early in the lives of their children. But there are some rare instances in which God waits until later in children's lives to save them. These exceptions are for His glory and the overall good of His people. They are not exceptions to the promise of salvation; they are exceptions to the normal time frame in which God fulfills His promise. God keeps His promises, though sometimes later than expected or even after a parent's death. He will not fail to make good on His word.

4. *If there is such a family-related promise, why is it not often taught in evangelical churches today?* I see three basic reasons why this teaching has fallen on hard times. The main reason for today's ignorance of God's promises to families is a lack of faithful teaching and modeling. Those who received this precious heritage have not been faithful in passing it on to their children. Some are too busy. Others are selfish or lazy. Some pastors and teachers become reluctant to pass on what they have not exemplified in their own homes. For whatever reason, truth can be lost when it is not faithfully taught, defended, and followed. The Holy Spirit is the Spirit of truth, and He is grieved when God's truth is forsaken for any reason.

Another reason why this teaching has been abandoned by many is a misunderstanding of why the major Protestant Reformers continued to practice infant baptism after they left the Roman Catholic Church. Many Christians today regard infant baptism as an ungodly remnant of Roman Catholicism, a relic of unbelief that the Reformers clung to when they broke from Rome. That is what I was taught when I was a young Christian. But few who accept that argument understand why infant baptism was and continues to be practiced by many Bible-believing evangelicals. Those of us who do baptize infants are firmly convinced, as were the Reformers, that the Scriptures support that view.

Christians who reject infant baptism tend also to reject the whole teaching of God's family covenant. But it is possible to embrace the promises of God for one's family without believing in infant baptism. A growing number of Baptists today are experiencing a renewal of understanding of the family covenant and are dedicating their children to the Lord as infants during their public worship services. I hope that this book will encourage that trend.

Though I firmly believe in infant baptism when rightly practiced, I will not deal with that question in this book, as that is not my purpose here. And so, even if you heartily disagree with me on that issue, I hope that we can agree on the clear promises of God's Word concerning the salvation of our children. Since we who are born again by faith in Jesus are brothers and sisters in Him, I write this book out of love for you and your family, whatever your denominational affiliation. Please do not allow traditional differences concerning baptism to keep you from exploring God's promises and applying them to your family.

Another reason for the neglect of God's family promises, in my opinion, is that some dispensationalist brothers have minimized the covenant workings of God. The word *covenant* became a distasteful word to many early dispensationalists. As a consequence, many good Christians spurned anything associated with covenant terminology. God's covenant promises to parents for their children fell victim to this aversion. I am hoping that more and more Christians will see that no one has the right to silence God's promises to parents concerning their children.

These are a few reasons why the teaching of this book is rarely heard in evangelical churches today. Though this precious truth has nearly been lost, thank God for revival! In the past, a revival of knowledge has often led to a revival of practice. Today, by God's grace, we can be part of a rediscovery of God's promises concerning our children and dedicate ourselves anew to raising them biblically. May the faithful promises of God grant Christian parents hope and help until Jesus returns.

Acknowledgments

I must first thank God for my obedient and faithful parents, in whose lives I saw and from whom I learned much of what I am sharing in this book.

Next, I want to thank my good friends Al and Margaret Swauger for initially urging me to write this book. And once that decision was made, my wife, children, mother, and parents-in-law gave unceasing prayer and encouragement that aided me in pursuing and completing the project.

I am grateful to the entire Van Eyk family for their special assistance. From purchasing a computer system for me, setting it up, typing, editing and suggesting, and calling me to offer encouragement and get updates, to calling the publisher and especially praying—they have all been vital helpers in the process of making this book a reality.

Several others have helped in proofreading and offering their invaluable suggestions for improving my very rough manuscript: my wife Debby, Dr. Robert Peterson, Mr. George Clark, Dr. Robert Styer, and my brother Strother Gross.

A special word of thanks goes to Mr. Thom Notaro of P&R Publishing for his patient and brotherly guidance in refining my manuscript and helping me to develop as a writer. Most publishers would not have dedicated the time and effort to me and this project that Thom has graciously given.

I also want to thank Mrs. Barbara Lerch, also of P&R, for her personal encouragement and support in bringing this book to print.

❖ PART ONE ❖

Our Dilemma

❖ Chapter One ❖

Questions from a Parent's Heart

We love our children. We hold them in our arms and dream about their future. At times our minds get carried away with what could be, until reality comes rushing in to interrupt our dreams. Oh that our dreams for our children's well-being would come true! What would we give to secure a good future for them, a future blessed by God? Is there anything we wouldn't offer for such a prize?

I want to encourage you to dream in the best interests of your children. Furthermore, I want to assure you that such dreams are good. It was Jesus who said that "you . . . being evil, know how to give good gifts to your children" (Matt. 7:11). He did not deride the natural desire of parents to do good for their children or regard those longings as selfishness. Instead, He honored parents' desires by showing that His Father has the same desire for His children: "If you then, being evil, know how to give good gifts to your children, how much more shall your

3

Father who is in heaven give what is good to those who ask Him!" (v. 11). So let us dream big dreams and pray big prayers for our children. God understands our feelings.

From our own experiences we parents have some idea of what lies ahead of our children, and we want to prepare them for it. We do not want them to repeat the blunders that have hurt us. And we are eager for them to learn quickly the important lessons that have helped us. There is nothing wrong with such godly desires. But are our hopes for our children achievable? Is our longing that they be blessed by God attainable? Can we ever be certain that our hearts' desires for our children will be achieved? Or are our wishes only a dream?

Before my wife and I had children, we discussed these things. We wanted to serve the Lord every day of our lives. We prayed that the Lord would use us to bring Him as much glory as a husband and wife could (and we still pray the same prayer today). Observing many Christian couples whose lives were devastated by troubles with their children, we seriously wondered, Is it God's will that our lives and ministry be jeopardized by a child who may forsake the ways of God and bring chaos into our home? To leave this question unanswered was unthinkable. What satisfaction would arise from our raising children who might gain the whole world but lose their own souls? We wondered: Can we know with any certainty that our children will love the Lord? Or must we live alongside them, through all the years of their development, haunted by the specter of their rejecting God or His rejecting them?

Debby and I went further: How can we bring a child into this life who may spend eternity in hell? Would we not be happier going through life alone, serving those around us, than giving birth to a child who might spend eternity separated from the Lord? These were real struggles we faced. And we knew that many other Christian couples and parents were facing the same dilemma. So we began to study. This book is the result of both that study and our efforts to apply what we have learned in raising four children for God.

Have you ever wondered, Does God love my children?

Does His Word reveal that He desires to save them? Has He declared what my duty as a parent is? Can I have assurance that my children will not fall away and end up in hell? Is there any way I can keep them from following the world? Can my prayers for them *really* make a difference? Well, I hope that through this book you will discover that God has answered these questions. And His answer is *yes!* So pray as you read this book that God will give you faith to believe and obey His Word. I hope that nothing will keep you from receiving the promises of God for your family, "for He who promised is faithful" (Heb. 10:23).

Discussion Questions

1. What are your greatest dreams for your children right now?
2. List some of the dreams that God has fulfilled in your life.
3. List some unfulfilled dreams that you have for your children and discuss why they might be unfulfilled.
4. How many Christian families around you are experiencing serious problems with their children? Do you see this trend increasing or decreasing?

Chapter Two

From Doubts to Convictions

It was a pivotal point in my life. I was working in a once-prestigious institution and could not believe some of the unethical practices occurring in administrative areas. I told the leaders of the institution, "I can no longer advise students to come to the place where I am teaching." Certainly that would get their attention, I thought. It did—but not in the way I had hoped. The president was not even interested in discussing the matter with me and sent a letter of dismissal to me that afternoon! Maybe I should have kept quiet. I began to question the wisdom of having raised the issue. If God was pleased with what I had done, would I have been fired? What was going to happen to my family? My mind was in turmoil.

In my hours of weakness and indecision, the Holy Spirit reminded me of a text I had memorized: "For we can do nothing against the truth, but only for the truth" (2 Cor. 13:8). How comforting that portion of God's Word was to Debby and me! Nothing can ultimately prevail against truth, because the God who is in control honors truth. We knew that God would not fail us, even though we had some huge obstacles before us.

We were told to vacate the premises, and we had no way to pay for adequate housing elsewhere. I did not know what to do, but I did know that what I had done was right because I had spoken the truth in love.

We often "reminded" God of that verse as we prayed that He would lead our family to where we could bring Him the most glory. An invitation to teach at a Bible college in the Far East came. We had done missionary work in Africa, so moving abroad again was not a major obstacle. Everyone was willing to make the move, and so we began planning for it. Then a close friend called us and said that he and his wife thought that we should serve the Lord in the U.S. instead of overseas. He asked if housing was a problem. When I replied that it was, he said, "You go look for a house that will serve your needs, pay what you can, and we will do the rest." These friends were not millionaires, but they had decided to take out a mortgage on their home in order to provide a home for us!

God proved to us that He will stand behind His Word and provide a way of escape when we cannot see one. He sometimes even gives us two great options. After prayer, we decided to stay for now in the U.S. And the Lord has graciously opened up a wonderful ministry for us. By the way, the institution I left has declined dramatically, removed most of its faculty, and sold off many of its belongings. I shudder to think of where I would be if I had taken the easy way out and kept silent. It is humbling to remember the number of times I considered doing just that. How often I have retold the story and left out any account of my weakness! Near sleeplessness and anxiety were the norm for a couple of weeks. My faith was not even that of a mustard seed. But God was so faithful, and a few Christian friends were extremely kind.

Will We Trust God?

Looking back on those events I marvel at the anxiety we need-lessly suffered. Because of unbelief, we were wrestling when we could have been resting. Jesus said, "My peace I give to you. . . . Let not your heart be troubled, nor let it be fearful" (John 14:27). I did not have to squirm or second-guess my decision to speak up. But unfortunately I did. I could have entrusted all the results to God and experienced peace. But during those troubling days I took my eyes off Him.

I realize now that I was not the only one affected by my unbelief. I wonder how many hurting people went unnoticed around me? How many unique opportunities to witness did I forfeit because I was absorbed in trying to figure out what was going to happen in *my* life? Though Isaiah said, "You will keep him in perfect peace, whose mind is stayed on You, because he trusts in You" (Isa. 26:3, NKJV), I didn't have perfect peace because my mind was fixed on my "problem." That "problem" was actually God's doorway to blessing, as are all problems that take us by surprise (see James 1:2–3). But why do we so rarely see the trying situations that we're going through as God's work? One reason is that our faith is weak. We simply do not trust God with all our heart.

We often eliminate God from our minds while we are at work, and yet we wonder why our jobs are so unfulfilling. We neglect His Word for guiding our families and are amazed at the bedlam that exists under our roofs. We carry our own burdens and are startled when our physical health breaks down— rising blood pressure, headaches, depression. Why do we torture ourselves by not trusting in God? Three reasons come to mind: (1) we don't know what God has said, (2) we don't see doubt as a bad thing, and (3) we have too few convictions. Let's turn our attention to each of these three areas and see how they affect our trusting the Lord.

What Must We Know?

There is much about God that we do not know. That should not surprise us since He is infinite and we are finite. What did God do for all eternity before He created the world? Why did He provide salvation for fallen men and not for fallen angels? Why was I born when and where I was born? When is Jesus going to return? Why did I have two sons and no daughters? Why was that child born with a permanent disability? Theologians call such concerns "the secret things of God." Many of us speculate on these things. Instead we need the humility of David, who determined, "O Lord, my heart is not proud, nor my eyes haughty; nor do I involve myself in great matters, or in things too difficult for me" (Ps. 131:1).

Although we too often wonder about the unknowable things—the "whys" of life—we either ignore or forget the many things that God has clearly revealed to us in His Word. In this, as in so many ways, our sinful natures are drawn to the darkness rather than the light. We proudly crave the knowledge that belongs only to God but reject the knowledge that matters most to our lives. Moses said, "The secret things belong to the Lord our God, but the things revealed belong to us and to our sons forever" (Deut. 29:29). The secret things and the revealed things ought to be kept distinct in our thinking. The things that God has not chosen to reveal belong to Him and therefore are not vital for our lives. The things that He has spoken are to be cherished, remembered, and obeyed. These are the things we must know.

God's Word is a "lamp to [our] feet and a light to [our] path" (Ps. 119:105). We are to live our lives according to it. What should we do in various situations? How should we act? What can we expect from God? from Satan? from mankind? from our children? Where should we go first for answers to these questions? To our culture? To human experts? No, the answers are in the Word of God. The Bible is so full of practical instruction that Jesus said that we could actually pattern our lives by it. He declared, "Man shall not live on bread alone, but on every word that proceeds out of the mouth of God" (Matt. 4:4). No area of human life is omitted from the divine counsel that God has graciously given. So, the Word of God is a sufficient guide for our lives. Paul wrote, "All Scripture is inspired by God and profitable . . . that the man of God may be adequate, equipped for every good work" (2 Tim. 3:16–17). Our problem is not a lack of information but a lack of knowledge and application!

Your family is important to God. He is the One who created the whole concept of the family. He said, "It is not good for the man to be alone" (Gen. 2:18). Thus He established the first family. And He has not abandoned families but has graciously provided them with a survival manual. The Bible is loaded with promises and principles from God for our families, and they all are trustworthy. The promises that God gives to believing parents cannot fail! But we must know them and do our part. If we are ignorant of God's promises, we can never claim them. In other words, we can't believe what we do not know. We must have knowledge of something before we can have faith in it. God's Word supplies for us the knowledge of the truth.

Satan understands this connection between knowledge and faith. He has been successful in blinding the minds of many, keeping them from comprehending and claiming the promises of God for their families. The results have been devastating. All around us we see the carnage of spiritually broken homes. Believers' children have no interest in the Lord, no regard for spiritual things. Many times they flaunt immoral behavior in the presence of their parents. Is this God's way? Is it His will for you? Must we accept this awful condition? God's Word says *no!* There is a better way; there is hope for your family. You are reading this book because you want to know what God has said to parents. But once you learn what He has said, how will you respond? Will you believe or doubt?

Is Doubt All That Bad?

Another hindrance to trusting God is doubt. The first words of Satan recorded in the Bible are, "Indeed, has God said . . . ?" (Gen. 3:1). Spreading doubt in our minds is a tactic the Evil One never seems to grow tired of. It's a far more vicious and harmful ploy than most of us realize. He loves to prey on our fragile minds by introducing questions of doubt regarding God's promises. And if we will follow, Satan will lead us down his path through doubt. As it was for our first parents in the Garden, so it will be for us—a pathway leading to destruction. We must recognize, then, that families can be destroyed by doubting parents.

Part of our problem is that we underestimate how bad doubt is. Doubting God's promises is not an innocent mental exercise—it is sin! Doubt is the opposite of faith, and "whatever is not from faith is sin" (Rom. 14:23). Every doubt is an act of rebellion against King Jesus. It questions His wisdom and control. Why do we doubt Him? Has He lost control? Has He failed us? Often we are too impatient to wait for Him to rescue us. We try instead to save ourselves.

Think of how important faith is, and you'll better understand how deadly doubt is. Salvation from sin and death comes through faith alone (Eph. 2:8–9). "Without faith it is impossible to please Him" (Heb. 11:6). We as Christians are commanded to "walk by faith, not by sight" (2 Cor. 5:7). By faith we overcome the world (1 John 5:4). Without faith we fall. Doubt and faith are irreconcilable enemies. So, where doubt grows, faith diminishes. And when faith grows weak, Satan's lies seem more plausible than God's promises.

How many of you are full of despair because you have no faith in what God can do for you and your children? Your faith seems so weak, and your doubts so strong. I pray that this book will help you to resist the doubt and instead "have faith in God" (Mark 11:22).

Where Are Our Convictions?

The more I think about my parents, the more amazed I am at the big decisions they made with little apparent anxiety. Decisions that would tie many of us in knots today, they made with tremendous peace. How did they do it? I think it was a result of their simple faith in God's Word. The Bible was the bottom line in our home. If Scripture said that something should be done or shouldn't be done, the issue was settled. There was no debate—God's Word should be followed, whatever the cost.

Sometimes the cost was great. I vividly remember Dad and Mom telling my younger brothers and me that they were going to send us to a Christian school. We didn't need to ask why, as they carefully led us through the same study of God's Word that had convinced them. Texts like Deuteronomy 6:4-9, 20-25; Psalm 78:1-8; and Ephesians 6:1-4 were read, and we listened carefully as they explained them to us.

There were three obstacles, however. The first was my unbelieving grandparents. They were ardent supporters of the public school system. Each marking period they gave cash gifts to several students throughout the town who excelled academically. Furthermore, my grandmother had been a teacher in the school. For her son to pull her grandsons out of her school would be an embarrassment and a disgrace. The shame would be magnified by his putting us into a Christian school. They put immense pressure on my parents to change their minds. But my parents didn't fold under the pressure. You see, there was no question in my parents' minds. The matter was nonnegotiable. They had developed a conviction from God's Word that their sons should not be educated by ungodly teachers in a system promoting anti-Christian values. They loved their parents, but they loved God even more.

I was the second obstacle. I was in the tenth grade, and God had blessed me with special athletic skills. I was starting on the varsity football team and had already been contacted by major universities concerning possible scholarships. The Christian school was too small for a football program. But I cannot remember objecting when Dad shared his desire with me. You see, I knew that it wasn't only Dad's will, but that it was also God's will. My dad liked to watch his sons play football as much as we enjoyed playing it. But personal preference has to be sacrificed sometimes to fulfill God's will. Receiving a Bible-centered education and developing Christian friendships were more important to him than the glory of his son's athletic accomplishments. Today I have an athletic son, and my dad's convictions mean more to me than ever.

The third obstacle was the location of the Christian school. It was about forty miles away from our home. Instead of causing the whole family to suffer from long trips, my parents decided to sell their beautiful home, move into a mobile home within walking distance of the school, and have Dad commute eighty miles per day to work. I cannot remember my dad ever complaining about his sacrifice. He was convinced that the benefits of their decision far outweighed the inconveniences.

He was right. The truths I learned and the experiences I had in those two years in a Christian high school changed the direction of my life. Today my wife and I have placed our children in Christian schools. Why? Not because it is easy; it is financially tough. We sacrifice because we believe that Mom and Dad were right in their conclusions about what Scripture says concerning education. I understand that there are situations in which formal Christian education doesn't seem possible. But where there's a will, there is usually a way. Christian parents bonding together in prayer can accomplish much. When Christian education becomes a conviction, parents will explore every possibility to make it a reality for their children.

Some Christian authors have made a helpful distinction between beliefs and convictions. Beliefs are truths that we affirm. For instance, I believe that the planet Pluto exists. This is my *belief*. Convictions, however, are those basic principles for which we are willing to sacrifice, suffer, and die. It is my *conviction* that the Word of God is truth. I could not deny this conviction without rejecting my entire view of life. Our beliefs may or may not greatly affect our behavior. I doubt that I would be willing to suffer for the belief that Pluto exists. But convictions determine behavior. They are deeply woven into a person's worldview (philosophy of life) and stand as the foundation of his or her life. Convictions are nonnegotiable. They hold the essence of life.

One of the problems with many Christians today is that they have very few convictions. The word *must* is not often used in reference to our spiritual duties. They are commonly viewed as optional rather than as essential. Most will say that they *believe* that the Bible is the authoritative Word of God. But few seem to actually *live* by its precepts. The Bible is a wonderful book to believe in, but when its principles cost us too dearly, we have a tendency to modify or reject them. We desperately need convictions today. And one basic conviction should be this: If the Bible teaches me to do something, by God's grace I will do it. It was because of their convictions that my parents chose to sacrifice their time, money, relationships, and comfort. But people without convictions cave in under the pressures of life and refuse to follow God.

The purpose of the following chapters is to set forth the knowledge of God's will for Christian families. God's promises and our responsibilities will both receive emphasis. I will aim to establish beyond question that God wants to save the children of believers and that He has revealed a way in which that is to be accomplished. I pray that any doubt you might have will be removed and that this wonderful truth will become a conviction in your life. Make no mistake, this is no small matter. How you respond to what you read will affect both you and future generations.

The good in store for families of those who embrace God's promises as convictions is incalculable. Likewise, the sorrow that awaits those who ignore God's promises for their families can be staggering. Great good or enormous evil is before you. A family torn by strife and spiritual chaos is *not* God's will for you. Why, then, are so many professing Christians allowing this horrible condition to ruin their homes? Many, sadly, do not know better. Some, crippled by doubt, wonder if God can really make a difference in their situations. Others are simply too selfish to pay the price that God's Word demands of believing parents. They opt to fill their Christianity with beliefs rather than convictions.

Biblical convictions have always demanded sacrifice in a world darkened by sin and selfishness. As the Master sacrificed and suffered for His convictions, so must His servants. There is no other way. He told us to walk a narrow and little-traveled path. He reminded us, however, that this path leads to life (Matt. 7:14). Though the promises of God to parents demand much of us, they lead to unbelievable blessing. They are a great gift to us and to our children.

God can be trusted to do within our families all that He has promised to do. As we examine the Scriptures, let us be full of faith and hope, knowing that it is impossible for God to lie (Heb. 6:18; Titus 1:2). Yes, God can be trusted! He will do just what He has said He would. And you will be truly blessed if you put your trust in Him.

Discussion Questions

1. Have you lived this week as though God can be trusted?
2. Why do we struggle to trust God in the midst of problems? What are three reasons for this?
3. Discuss the differences between the secret and the revealed things of God. What happens when we switch our focus from the revealed to the secret will of God?
4. Discuss why doubt is such a dangerous sin. What are some ways in which Satan sows doubt in your mind?
5. Explain the difference between beliefs and convictions. What are some of your convictions?

❖ PART TWO ❖

Our Discovery

❖ Chapter Three ❖

"You and Your Children"

Debby and I were sitting at our table talking with a couple of our missionary friends. They were expressing amazement at the number of missionary families they knew who were having serious problems with their children, problems of unbelief and ungodliness. Because they knew of so many examples, our friends seemed to accept that such problems are a normal part of the missionary's life in today's world, that they go with the turf of serving God and being under attack by the Devil.

When we disagreed, saying that unbelief or rebellion by children of believers is neither right nor inevitable, the conversation grew intense. The topic involved people very close to them, and so they expressed initial resistance and resentment concerning what we were saying. But the more we read God's Word, the more open our friends became. After a long discussion one of them remarked: "I have never heard that before. You ought to write a book on it because it would be a great help to a lot of people."

I was extremely busy in ministry at the time, but that night I tossed and turned because of the challenge I had been given. As I prayed, I knew what I should do. I knew there was a need, and the Bible teaches that if our fellow Christians have a need, we should do whatever we can to help them. Anything less is not loving our neighbors as ourselves. And since I love you, my brothers and sisters, I have been compelled to write this book for you and your children.

In this and the next two chapters I will lay out what God has promised to you and your family. Following that, I will examine what God expects us to do in faith as Christian parents. Please try to keep an open mind as you read the verses I present. Ask yourself at the close of each chapter if I have been fair with God's Word. I am not writing this to attack parents or to expose them to ridicule. My hope is that we all will know better what God desires for our families. So, no matter how close to home this study gets, or how painful for you, follow it through to the end, and respond as the Spirit leads. I want all of my brothers and sisters to know that if they are having family problems, God is on their side. They do not have to give up, for God promises to help.

The Promise in Acts

Acts 2:36–39

> "Therefore let all the house of Israel know for certain that God has made Him both Lord and Christ—this Jesus whom you crucified." Now when they heard this, they were pierced to the heart, and said to Peter and the rest of the apostles, "Brethren, what shall we do?" And Peter said to them, "Repent and let each of you be baptized in the name of Jesus Christ for the forgiveness of your sins; and you shall receive the gift of the Holy Spirit. For the promise is for you and your children, and for all who are far off, as many as the Lord our God shall call to Himself."

What a great moment that was in the history of the church. After Peter's message thousands were convinced that Jesus was God's Son and that they had consented to His death. So they cried out, "What shall we do?" They wanted to know how they could be saved from their dreadful plight. Peter gave them a clear answer and a wonderful promise from the same God they had previously resisted and offended. Forgiveness of sins was possible even for those who had crucified the Messiah—if they would repent. This was truly good news for troubled souls.

Peter expressed the promise of salvation to those first-century Jews with the words, "You shall receive the gift of the Holy Spirit." God does not give His Spirit in this promised way to anyone except His forgiven children. The gift of the Spirit is the gift of new birth, without which no one can enter God's kingdom (John 3:5).

But Peter knew that his listeners were not concerned only for themselves; they were also concerned for their children. And rightly so, because when they rejected the Messiah, they implicated their children in their dreadful act. According to Matthew, Pilate "took water and washed his hands in front of the multitude, saying, 'I am innocent of this Man's blood.'" At that moment "all the people answered and said, 'His blood be on us and our children!'" (Matt. 27:24–25). Their entire history taught them that the actions of parents affected their children. But they were assured by their religious leaders that Jesus was a fraud. Little did they know, when they spoke those words, that they were calling God's curse on themselves and their children.

To these worried sinners Peter spoke comforting words when he said, "For the promise is for *you and your children*" (Acts 2:39). What promise was Peter talking about? Well, what were the people crying out for? They were crying out for salvation, for cleansing from their sin. They were told how the promised work of the Holy Spirit could influence their lives. The promise offered to those repenting sinners was the promise of salvation. And the same promise was extended to their children, too.

It was not unusual for New Testament writers to speak of salvation as "the promise of the Spirit," as Peter did when addressing the crowd in Jerusalem. Paul wrote of salvation coming "to the Gentiles, so that we might receive *the promise of the Spirit* through faith" (Gal. 3:14). He represented all believers as being "sealed in [Christ] with *the Holy Spirit of promise*" (Eph. 1:13). That is what Peter was saying on the Day of Pentecost. He was telling his hearers how they and their children could be saved by the power of the Holy Spirit.

So the promise of salvation was extended to believers and their children in Peter's first message, recorded in Acts. Was this promise only for *them*? Or does it continue to be in effect today? Why shouldn't the promise be limited to that crowd alone? Why shouldn't Christians of all ages possess the same promise that salvation is offered to them and to their children? Satan would love for us to doubt that God's promises apply to us. But to counter that doubt, the Holy Spirit urged Peter to say, "The promise is for you and your children, *and for all who are far off*, as many as the Lord our God shall call to Himself." That promise was not only a Jewish promise, confined to those then present. It was a universal promise made to all everywhere whom God would call to salvation. The Gentiles were those who were "far off" (Eph. 2:13, 17), and so the promise is for you and me just as much as for those who first heard it.

It is significant that the very first presentation of the gospel in Acts offers salvation to believing parents *and* to their children. Is this offer repeated anywhere else in Scripture? If such a promise were found only once, some might try to cast doubt on its relevance to us. But to remove all doubt, the Lord has revealed it many times and in many ways, one of which occurs later in Acts.

Acts 16:29–31

> And he called for lights and rushed in and, trembling with fear, he fell down before Paul and Silas, and after he brought them out, he said, "Sirs, what must I do to be saved?" And they said, "Believe in the Lord Jesus, and you shall be saved, you and your household."

What a promise was made to the Philippian jailer! Not only would he be saved, but the promise of salvation was extended to his entire household—if he believed. How often have you heard Acts 16:31 quoted without the end of the verse? "Believe on the Lord Jesus, and you shall be saved." The four closing words have been ripped away as though they pertained only to that man and had no application to the rest of humanity. Who has the right to cut out those words? What expert, what theologian, what preacher has a right to thus limit the promises of God?

Satan does not want us to believe that God loves our families or has made promises concerning their salvation and blessing. But why would God make such a promise to the jailer alone? He didn't. And this is not the only text in which the promise of household salvation is given. Nor was Paul the only one to give such a promise.

Other New Testament Texts

Peter expressed the same truth when he proclaimed the gospel to Cornelius, the first gentile convert to Christianity. An angel appeared to Cornelius and said, "Send to Joppa, and have Simon, who is also called Peter, brought here; and he shall speak words to you by which you will be saved, *you and all your household*" (Acts 11:13–14).

God sent an angel to communicate to Cornelius the fact that the promise of salvation was not only for him, but for his entire family. Peter had given the promise of salvation to Jewish believers and their children on the Day of Pentecost. The same promise was extended to the Gentile Cornelius. God's message of saving love reaches out to all the families of the earth, Jewish and non-Jewish alike. I don't believe that God loved Cornelius more than he loves any other believer. He wants the best for your family too and has made a way for that to happen in your life—if you will cast off doubt and believe.

The writers of the New Testament understood that God

worked through the families of believers. And they made note of it. Their inspired history of Christianity repeatedly bears witness to God's grace upon believers' households. Each of the following accounts relates specific blessings brought upon the families of believers:

- of the royal official (John 4:53);
- of the people at Pentecost (Acts 2:39);
- of Cornelius (Acts 11:14);
- of Lydia (Acts 16:15);
- of the Philippian jailer (Acts 16:31–33);
- of Crispus, the leader of the synagogue at Corinth (Acts 18:8);
- of Stephanus (1 Cor. 1:16);
- of Onesiphorus (2 Tim. 1:16; 4:19).

Take the time to read these accounts. These households are not mentioned arbitrarily. Through them God gives us the assurance that He will work in our families too, if we will follow their faithful example.

Some Old Testament Texts

The entire New Testament was not available for common use to first-century Christians. So what guided their daily lives? The Old Testament, of course (see 2 Tim. 3:14–17). Paul reminded the believing Romans that the Old Testament was "written for our instruction" (Rom. 15:4). Christians today, therefore, can and should still benefit greatly from the Old Testament.

When we study the Old Testament, it is not long before we discover that God's will is to save and bless the families of believers. In the course of this book we will look at what God revealed in both Testaments to parents concerning their children. Right now we want to mention only a few texts that promise salvation to the children of believing and obedient parents.

Genesis 17:7

> And I will establish My covenant between Me and you
> and your descendants after you throughout their gen-
> erations for an everlasting covenant, to be God to you
> and to your descendants after you.

Abraham believed God, and God blessed him. God made
a covenant or solemn agreement with Abraham that included
many things. The promise most relevant to our study is the
promise of salvation to his descendants. When God vowed to be
"God to you and to your descendants after you," He was prom-
ising salvation to Abraham and his descendants. Few would
disagree with that. But who are Abraham's descendants who
possess this "everlasting covenant"? Does it apply to us?

The New Testament makes it explicitly clear that all born-
again Christians are Abraham's descendants. Paul wrote, "Therefore, be sure that it is those who are of faith who are sons of
Abraham. . . . So then those who are of faith are blessed with
Abraham, the believer. . . . And if you belong to Christ, then you
are Abraham's offspring, *heirs according to promise*" (Gal. 3:7, 9,
29).

Paul's words were written to converted Gentiles. How
could a Gentile be a descendant of Abraham, the father of
the Jews? The answer is that salvation through faith makes
one a child of Abraham. Paul explains, "For he is not a Jew
who is one outwardly; neither is circumcision that which is
outward in the flesh. But he is a Jew who is one inwardly;
and circumcision is that which is of the heart, by the Spirit"
(Rom. 2:28–29).

I am amazed at how many people accept the first part of
God's promise in Genesis 17:7 but ignore or reject the second
part. We believe that God will be a God to us but doubt that He
will be a God to our descendants after us. Both promises should
be embraced by a living faith. We have the right to claim both
promises and to be assured of our children's future salvation
just as we can be assured of our present salvation. God has

graciously made an agreement with believing parents to stand in the same relationship with their children as He does with them. Shall we leave that promise unclaimed? Listen carefully to these words written long ago by Andrew Murray (1828–1917) concerning this promise:

> The *condition* of the promise is in each case the same. In its twofold blessing it is offered to *the faith* of the parent, and has to be accepted by faith alone. If the promise, *"I will be thy God"* be not believed, that unbelief makes the promise of none effect. God is true, His promise faithful, His offer of mercy real. But if it finds no entrance through unbelief, the blessing is lost. And so with the other half, *"a God to thy seed";* if the parent's faith accepts this for his child, God will see to it that his faith is not disappointed. (*How to Raise Your Children for Christ,* 36)

So, God promised salvation to both Abraham and his descendants. He said that He would be their God. And this relationship was called an "everlasting covenant." It still continues today because the New Testament calls both gentile and Jewish believers "Abraham's descendants" and "heirs according to promise." We stand together with Abraham, as Paul wrote, "in order that in Christ Jesus the blessing of Abraham might come to the Gentiles, so that we might receive *the promise of the Spirit through faith"* (Gal. 3:14). The full blessing of Abraham is ours, including not only our salvation but also the promise of our children's salvation—if we truly believe.

Deuteronomy 30:6, 19

> Moreover the LORD your God will circumcise your heart and the heart of your descendants, to love the LORD your God with all your heart and with all your soul, in order that you may live. . . . I call heaven and earth to witness against you today, that I have set

before you life and death, the blessing and the curse.
So choose life in order that you may live, you and your
descendants.

The promise of circumcising one's heart and the hearts of
one's descendants is the promise of salvation. The circumcision
of the heart is the regenerating work of the Holy Spirit (Deut.
10:16; Jer. 4:4; Ezek. 36:26–27). What is promised in this text,
then, is nothing less than the salvation of certain people and
their descendants. Here again we see the heart of our unchang-
ing God. It is His express desire to bless not only us but also our
children after us. He is a God of great love and mercy to His
children.

Deuteronomy 31:13

And their children, who have not known, will hear
and learn to fear the LORD your God, as long as you
live on the land which you are about to cross the
Jordan to possess.

In common Old Testament terminology, a believer is one
who fears the Lord. In Deuteronomy 31:13, God shows how
the children of faithful Jews could come to fear the Lord,
that is to say, be saved. So, the promise that God made
through Moses to the children of Israel was a promise of salvation for their future, unborn children. That promise was
conditional. The parents were to continue to live in Israel
and follow the Word of their God. We know that Israel did
not keep their part of the deal and subsequently went into
bondage. But Israel's unbelief did not nullify the legitimacy
and power of God's promises. The promises were true, yet
unclaimed. Because they were conditional promises, demand-
ing faith of the Israelites, they were not fulfilled as they could
have been. And what was true in that day is likewise true
today. The promises remain, but they are doubted and dis-
carded by many Christians.

Psalm 103:17–18

> But the lovingkindness of the LORD is from everlasting
> to everlasting on those who fear Him, and His right-
> eousness to children's children, to those who keep His
> covenant, and who remember His precepts to do them.

Here is a promise of salvation to the children of those who
believe and act accordingly. God's righteousness, a perfect righteousness, is promised to their children and even to their grandchildren. When God's righteousness is imputed to someone, he
or she becomes guiltless before God. The person is justified. In
these verses, God promises to give His righteousness to the
children and grandchildren of believers who understand and
obey His covenant with them. Those blessed children are not
saved on the basis of their parents' obedience. Rather, they are
saved through the agency of their parents. The grace of God is
the basis of salvation. From beginning to end, it is all of grace.
Even the faith believers have is theirs by God's grace!

For those who will receive it, then, there is a promise of
salvation to believers and their families. What was true in the
days of Abraham, Moses, and Solomon was true also for the
New Testament age of Peter and Paul. And why should that
seem strange? Isn't the New Testament particularly noted as
the beginning of grace for all peoples? It would indeed be
strange if God were less gracious to New Testament families
than He was to Old Testament families, wouldn't it? Why
should Christians today be robbed of the promises passed on
by the apostles to New Testament believers and their families?

Discussion Questions

1. What was the promise that Peter spoke of in Acts 2:39?
   Was it limited only to the Jewish listeners who heard him?
   Explain.

2. Why is it wrong to omit the last four words when quoting Acts 16:31?

3. Can you name any whole households of your acquaintance that have been blessed with salvation? What noticeable characteristics can you note that make these families different from others?

4. Are you a descendant of Abraham? Why or why not? If you are, what special promise has God made to you?

5. In your opinion, has today's preaching amply stressed God's promises to parents? What is the result for those parts of the church today in which these promises are not stressed? How should this omission be rectified?

❖ CHAPTER FOUR ❖

God Works Through Families

Ruth was wonderfully converted and wanted her husband immediately to turn to the Lord, too. But Ralph was not as anxious for this spiritual change as she thought he would be. He was the dentist of a small town in upstate New York with a nice home, fine cars, a summer cottage on the lake, and a respected place in society and his church. Why did *he* have to change? Maybe Ruth needed to be born again, but he thought his life was just fine as it was.

As Ruth studied the Bible, she grew quickly in faith and knowledge. Discovering that the Bible was full of promises, she began claiming these promises for her family and friends. Many were being converted. Her sons began showing real spiritual growth. But the biggest obstacle was Ralph—and at 6'5" and nearly three hundred pounds he was indeed big. For nine months she prayed specifically that God would save him and call him into full-time Christian service.

Ralph seemed invincible. Many people had witnessed to him. He had even allowed a Bible study, at which several were converted, to meet in their home. Moreover, he would occasionally attend church with Ruth. But still he seemed content, and Ruth saw precious time slipping away. In frustration one night she chose an article and began reading it to him. It was about a Christian husband with an unsaved wife. She thought it might make him aware of their spiritual division. Soon after beginning, however, Ruth looked over and discovered that Ralph was sound asleep.

Ruth knew that the Lord commands us to cast all our cares upon Him because He cares for us (1 Peter 5:7). So she finally and completely did just that. Through tears she told the Lord that Ralph's salvation was the greatest burden on her soul and that she could do nothing to change his heart. Handing him over to the Lord that night to work on him in His own way and in His own time, she gave up, rolled over, and fell asleep.

Later that same night Ralph was awakened from a sound sleep under immense conviction. With tears running down his cheeks he quietly knelt at the side of his bed and received Jesus Christ as his Lord and Savior. From that moment Ralph was never the same. He began witnessing for Christ through his dental practice. But soon that wasn't enough. He decided to go on a short-term missionary trip to Africa. There he and one of his sons spent three months serving the Lord through dentistry and preaching. Not long afterwards Ralph and Ruth decided to sell their home and his dental practice in order to become full-time medical missionaries in Africa. They enjoyed twelve years of serving Christ together in Africa until Ralph was taken home to heaven in 1985.

This story of prayer and transformation is very special to me. You see, Ralph and Ruth are my parents. I was the boy who accompanied his dad on his first missionary trip to Africa. My parents proved God's faithfulness before my very eyes. I heard their prayers, I heard them claim His promises—and time after time I saw Him wonderfully answer their prayers. Claiming God's promises in prayer is part of the heritage passed on to me by my precious parents.

God does work mightily through families who call on Him and trust in Him. In this chapter we will see how parents can positively or negatively affect their children. I will share a few biblical examples that clearly show that God desires to save whole families. I will also illustrate the fact that destruction often awaits those families whose parents do not choose to follow the Lord.

Old Testament Examples

Noah

In the days of Noah, the earth was so corrupt that God said, "I will blot out man whom I have created from the face of the land" (Gen. 6:7). However, Noah, being a righteous man, "found favor in the eyes of the LORD" (v. 8). What form did God's favor take? You may know the story, but have you considered how Noah's family was blessed through his faith? The Lord said:

> And behold, I, even I am bringing the flood of water upon the earth, to destroy all flesh in which is the breath of life, from under heaven; everything that is on the earth shall perish. But I will establish My covenant with you; and you shall enter the ark—*you and your sons and your wife, and your sons' wives with you.* (vv. 17–18)

What a blessing for Noah's family! The Lord said, "Enter the ark, *you and all your household;* for you alone I have seen to be righteous before Me in this time" (Gen. 7:1). The New Testament recalls this event: "By faith Noah, being warned by God about things not yet seen, in reverence prepared an ark *for the salvation of his household,* by which he condemned the world, and became an heir of the righteousness which is according to faith" (Heb. 11:7).

What are we doing for the salvation of our households? Do

we have the faith of Noah? Do we believe that the God of Noah is our God too and loves our families as He loved Noah's?

Lot

When God sent angels to destroy Sodom, they asked Lot urgently: "Whom else have you here? A son-in-law, and your sons, and your daughters, and whomever you have in the city, bring them out of this place" (Gen. 19:12). If God spares a man, He also seeks to spare the man's family. It is a sad thing that in the end only Lot and his two daughters were delivered. There was great failure—but not with God. And there are many who fail to receive the family blessings today, as we shall see, because they reject the conditions that God has established in His Word. Parents forsake their duties for many reasons. Like Lot, some choose what appears best materially (Gen. 13:10–11) and sadly lose their families in the process. When he tried to persuade his sons-in-law to leave with him, "He appeared to his sons-in-law to be jesting" (Gen. 19:14). That was Lot's tragic failure; his plight was not God's desire.

The Passover

> Then Moses called for the elders of Israel, and said to them, "Go and take for yourselves lambs according to your families, and slay the Passover lamb." (Ex. 12:21)

The Passover was one of the most solemn moments in the history of God's work on earth. He was about to deliver His children from Egyptian bondage. It was a time of life and death, grace and judgment: grace upon the believing families of Israel and judgment upon the unbelieving families of Egypt from Pharaoh down to his servants.

God stipulated what was necessary for the atonement of the sins of His people. No more and no less was required. What did the holy Lord demand? *One lamb for a family*. Not one lamb per person, but one lamb per family. As the father (or guardian) decided, so it went with the family. As Pharaoh and the fathers of Egypt decided, so it went with their families. God worked through families.

Later Moses reminded the children of Israel of the blessing derived from fathers when he said: "Because He loved your fathers, therefore He chose their descendants after them. And He personally brought you from Egypt by His great power" (Deut. 4:37). The Lord loved the fathers and chose their descendants. This has always been the way of the Lord. He shows His wondrous love to believing parents by blessing their children. He also reveals His awesome justice upon many families of those who reject His Word.

Mount Sinai

An example of both God's justice and His mercy visited on families is found in the Ten Commandments. Moses writes:

> You shall not make for yourself an idol. . . . You shall not worship them or serve them; for I, the LORD your God, am a jealous God, visiting the iniquity of the fathers on the children, on the third and the fourth generations of those who hate Me, but showing lovingkindness to thousands, to those who love Me and keep My commandments. (Ex. 20:4–6)

God may punish the sins of the wicked for as many as three or four generations. But Scripture portrays Him as more desirous of showing His love and grace. He will show mercy to thousands of generations of those who love Him. After Moses broke the tablets, and God passed in front of him to replace the tablets, He proclaimed,

> The LORD, the LORD God, compassionate and gracious, slow to anger, and abounding in lovingkindness and truth; who keeps lovingkindness for thousands, who forgives iniquity, transgression and sin; yet He

will by no means leave the guilty unpunished, visiting the iniquity of fathers on the children and on the grandchildren to the third and fourth generations. (Ex. 34:6–7)

God shows mercy to us sinners in that "Christ redeemed us from the curse of the Law, having become a curse for us" (Gal. 3:13). How thankful we should be for the sin-bearing death of Jesus Christ, which has removed the judgment of the broken law from our guilty heads! How blessed are all who walk by faith in His righteousness and bask in the full sunlight of God's grace extended so liberally to them and to their families.

Korah's Rebellion

Before we move on from God's judgment, let us soberly recall the dreadful consequences of Korah's rebellion. He and others had rebelled against the Word and authority of God, stirring up mutiny against Moses and Aaron. Consider carefully the consequences of the sin of those parents.

> Then Moses arose and went to Dathan and Abiram, with the elders of Israel following him, and he spoke to the congregation, saying, "Depart now from the tents of these wicked men, and touch nothing that belongs to them, lest you be swept away in all their sin." So they got back from around the dwellings of Korah, Dathan and Abiram; and Dathan and Abiram came out and stood at the doorway of their tents, *along with their wives and their sons and their little ones.* And Moses said, "By this you shall know that the LORD has sent me to do all these deeds; for this is not my doing. . . ." Then it came about as he finished speaking all these words, that the ground that was under them split open; and the earth opened its mouth and swallowed them up, *and their households,* and all the men that belonged to Korah, with their possessions. So

they and all that belonged to them went down alive to Sheol; and the earth closed over them, and they perished from the midst of the assembly. (Num. 16:25–33)

Scripture emphatically demonstrates that parents' lives bring either good or evil consequences upon their children. God gives us many illustrations of both blessings and judgments upon whole families because of the faith or disobedience of parents. That truth ought to drive us to our knees. Let us plead for His grace and ever look to Christ to fulfill all His promises of love and mercy. And let us also strive to be faithful in performing all our parental duties by His enabling grace.

New Testament Examples

In the New Testament we also see the principle of parents and children being treated as a unit. Blessings are given to or withheld from families as a result of the responses of parents to God's Word. In fact, Jesus told His disciples to operate on this principle in their relationships to both homes and cities. They were to place blessings on those homes and cities that welcomed them. Jesus added, however, "Whoever does not receive you, nor heed your words, as you go out of that house or that city, shake off the dust of your feet. Truly I say to you, it will be more tolerable for the land of Sodom and Gomorrah in the day of judgment, than for that city" (Matt. 10:14–15).

There would have been little children in these homes and cities. Think of the awful consequences they would suffer because of their parents' rejection of the truth—years of wandering in ignorance and darkness. But how blessed were those children whose fathers had welcomed the disciples of the Lord! That has always been the way of God.

Paul reflected the premise that God desires to bless believers' families when he prayed, "The Lord grant mercy to the house of Onesiphorus for he often refreshed me, and was not ashamed of my chains" (2 Tim. 1:16). I don't know what happened to Onesiphorus. Perhaps he was imprisoned or martyred. This I do know—Paul prayed that the family would be blessed because of the faithfulness of the father. To Paul such a prayer was not a presumption; it was natural because he knew the way God works His grace through families.

Is It Fair?

You might wonder if it is fair for God to allow parents' decisions to so dramatically affect their children. Well, if God does it, it must be fair! If He acts upon this principle, then it is a right and just principle, because "the Lord is righteous in all His ways" (Ps. 145:17).

The principle of representation occurs in both biblical and secular history. The sin of Adam affected not only himself but all who descended from him. The life and death of Christ affect not only Himself but all whom He represented. Paul wrote, "For as through the one man's disobedience the many were made sinners, even so through the obedience of the One the many will be made righteous" (Rom. 5:19). Those who reject the principle of representation, then, must reject the justice of God's wonderful plan of redemption, which is founded upon it.

When Jeremiah prayed, he addressed God as the One "who showest lovingkindness to thousands, but repayest the iniquity of fathers into the bosom of their children after them" (Jer. 32:18). Since God's nature does not change, we should expect that the Lord still continues to allow sin to run its awful course through successive generations. Charles Hodge summarizes the biblical teaching on this subject:

> The curse pronounced on Canaan fell upon his posterity. Esau's selling his birthright, shut out his descendants from the covenant of promise. . . . In the case of Dathan and Abiram, as in that of Achan, "their wives, and their sons, and their little children" perished [phys-

ically] for the sins of their parents. God said to Eli, that the iniquity of his house should not be purged with sacrifice and offering forever. To David it was said, "The sword shall never depart from thy house; because thou hast despised me, and hast taken the wife of Uriah the Hittite to be thy wife." To the disobedient Gehazi it was said, "The leprosy of Naaman shall cleave unto thee and unto thy seed forever." . . . Our Lord himself said to the Jews of his generation that they built the sepulchres of the prophets whom their fathers had slain, and thus acknowledged themselves to be the children of murderers, and that therefore the blood of those prophets should be required at their hands. This principle runs through the whole of Scriptures. . . . No man who believes the Bible, can shut his eyes to the fact that it everywhere recognizes the representative character of parents, and that the dispensations of God have from the beginning been founded on the principle that children bear the iniquities of their fathers. (*Systematic Theology*, 2:198–99)

What is true of the Scriptures is no less true of human experience in general. Hodge adds:

The punishment of the felon involves his family in his disgrace and misery. The spendthrift and drunkard entail poverty and wretchedness upon all connected with them. There is no nation now existing on the face of the earth, whose condition (for good or evil) is not largely determined by the character and conduct of their ancestors. (Ibid., 199)

When the president declares war on a certain nation, do we act as if such a declaration does not exist? Do we travel to the other nation and declare that we disagree with the president's decision and seek to remain neutral? No, the president's authority is based upon the principle of representation. All the parliaments of the world operate on the same principle because their founders understood the justice behind representation.

The same is true of a family. Indeed, it is here that the principle is clearest. The helpless child is held in the parent's arms. The very character of the parent is communicated to that child in a million ways through birth and upbringing. The child becomes what he or she experiences and sees. Softness of speech, gentleness, and a spirit of gratitude are normally passed on by soft-spoken, gentle, thankful parents. The rudeness, loudness, and abrasiveness of parents are likewise often mirrored in their children.

Parental responsibility is an awesome thing, deeply felt by every thinking parent who considers his or her "helpless infant." We cannot say that the principle of representation is wrong and throw it away because of the irresponsibility and selfishness of some parents. To reject this principle is to rebel against the very laws God has planted within us for the good order of all society.

There is so much stress today on individuals' rights, even children's rights, that this whole principle in regard to the family is being challenged. Parents are told that they have no right to try to influence their children morally or spiritually. It is the child's right to determine his or her own direction, some insist. We must stand on guard against the neutralizing of our convictions by the dictates of the surrounding ungodly culture. God still reigns. Happiness can never be achieved by rejecting the laws of our Creator. And representation is one of those laws. It will be either His way or confusion.

I want to clarify one point about the extent of a child's reaping what his parents have sown. This principle is unquestionably applicable in many areas of a child's life. And, as we have seen, the consequences of his parents' sin might even cost him his physical life. But it is important to understand that no one is condemned to eternal death by God and sent to hell for his or her parents' sins. Individual responsibility is clearly taught in Ezekiel 18:1–32 and elsewhere. Each person must stand before Him and give an account of himself.

So children are not condemned to hell for their parents' sin. And neither is anyone saved by virtue of his parents' obedience, however much he may benefit from it. God's grace alone is the foundation of salvation. And yet, if a child does not accept the way of salvation himself, he will not be saved.

But none of this voids the promises of God to parents for their children. They are to believe and claim them. If a parent understands God's loving desires for the salvation of his home and claims them, he is doing so *only by the grace of God*. If we train up our children in His way, that too is only by the grace of God. No one but God deserves glory in the redemption of sinners.

The Lord works His will through the families of mankind. Generation follows generation in succession. Blessings for obedience and consequences for sin are passed on from parent to child in unmistakable ways. Noah believed and obeyed the Lord, and his whole family was delivered. The former prostitute Rahab expressed faith in the God of Israel and safely housed the two spies when they visited Jericho (Josh. 2). She not only secured deliverance for her father's household but later married Salmon, gave birth to Boaz, and became one of the direct ancestors of the Messiah (Matt. 1:5)! Her children and parents were blessed because of her.

This principle of parental influence works negatively, too. Solomon certainly was influenced by his father's negative example. David's marriages to several wives and consorts (2 Sam. 5:13) not only weakened him and his kingdom but also gave precedent that led to his son's downfall. Solomon, so wise and good in many ways, indulged in the same sin as his father had. It was his many wives who "turned his heart away after their gods" (1 Kings 11:4). David supplied a devastating example for his son. What legacy will you pass on to your children and grandchildren? You are determining that by the way you live today.

Will you claim the following promises in Psalm 115 for you and your family today? I pray that God will give you the faith to do so and to continue clinging to them.

The LORD has been mindful of us; He will bless us; He will bless the house of Israel; He will bless the house of Aaron. He will bless those who fear the LORD, the small together with the great. May the LORD give you increase, you and your children. May you be blessed of the LORD, Maker of heaven and earth. (vv. 12–15)

Discussion Questions

1. Is the Bible your guide? Does it actually settle the great questions and debates of your life? Why or why not?
2. Which Old Testament example has most affected you? What principle can be derived from it for us today?
3. Do you have trouble accepting the principle of representation? Why or why not? What should determine what Christians accept or reject?
4. In your opinion what is the greatest legacy you can pass on to your children? Why?
5. Have you been blessed through your parents? Has your family been blessed through you? Discuss.

❖ CHAPTER FIVE ❖

"Only Believe"

I never met her, but she must have been one remarkable woman. Victoria was a faithful Christian wife and mother living in West Philadelphia. She was a woman of compassion and faith. Although she was disabled, she would feed many in her neighborhood and offer them Christian counsel through her window or while sitting on her porch. She also served the neighborhood through her prayers. Her son Sam was the special object of her prayers.

Sam loved his mother, but he also loved the world. So he ran with the world, trying to keep one step ahead of the law, the gangsters he owed money to, and his mother's persistent prayers. Eventually they all caught up with him.

Victoria died in 1969 without having seen her son turn to the Lord. When Sam asked about the sweet smile on her lifeless face, the undertaker said, "She died that way—we didn't give her that smile." How could she have such peace when so many of her prayers were unanswered? God's timing is often different from ours. Victoria knew that.

Sam ran harder and harder. He would go out the back

door when a preacher would come in the front. When Sam answered the door one day, standing before him were two thugs sent to collect what he owed their boss. Sam was weary of life and told the men to shoot him, because he did not have the money. He was amazed when they simply turned around and left. He had expected to die. He *wanted* to die.

Everything came to a head one day when he accidentally shot another man and became the object of a police manhunt. Sam ran and hid in a dumpster. Everything inside him said, *This is it! Jump out and shoot it out with them.* His heart was pounding. He opened the dumpster, but no shots rang out. He crawled out unnoticed by the police, and yet he couldn't run. His mother's prayers had caught up with him. He surrendered to the police and to the Lord.

Today, Sam is a very productive Christian and one of my most trusted counselors. He marvels at his mother's faith, a faith that led her simply to claim God's promises for her son and keep on praying when the world was tightening its stranglehold on him. He recently told me that three generations have been spiritually blessed by his mother's prayers. Victoria didn't let the ominous clouds of poverty and crime obscure her faith in the power of prayer. Nothing in her environment seemed to give her hope for her son—but she believed that God ruled over her environment, even West Philadelphia! So she refused to be victimized by doubt, trusted in the power of God, and brought untold blessings into the lives of others.

In this chapter we will see how the love of God and the life of Christ give further evidence of God's desire to work His grace in our homes in unique and wonderful ways. May the Lord help you, like Victoria, to cling to His promises and prove His faithfulness.

The Love of God

God is love (1 John 4:8). Every decree and act of God is bathed in infinite love. It is wrong to portray Him as indifferent, malevolent, or unkind. He is "good to all. And His mercies are over all His works" (Ps. 145:9). He is represented as desiring the salvation of all (1 Tim. 2:4), as "not wishing for any to perish but for all to come to repentance" (2 Peter 3:9). He was not deceiving us when He declared, "As I live! . . . I have no pleasure in the death of the wicked, but rather that the wicked turn from his way and live" (Ezek. 33:11); and, "Do I have any pleasure in the death of the wicked, . . . rather than that he should turn from his ways and live?" (Ezek. 18:23). As Jeremiah said, "He does not afflict willingly, or grieve the sons of men" (Lam. 3:33). Nor was Jesus misleading His hearers when He cried, "O Jerusalem, Jerusalem, who kills the prophets and stones those who are sent to her! How often I wanted to gather your children together, the way a hen gathers her chicks under her wings, and you were unwilling" (Matt. 23:37).

Commenting on these and other related texts, Charles Hodge said, "All these passages teach that God delights in the happiness of his creatures, and that when he permits them to perish, or inflicts evil upon them, it is from some inexorable necessity; that is, because it would be unwise and wrong to do otherwise" (*Princeton Sermons,* 19).

Do you think for a moment, dear Christian parent, that your heavenly Father desires your children to be lost? Should He be thought of as a God who saves parents and then plagues them with ungodly and rebelling children regardless of how faithful those parents are? No! We must not permit such a misconception even to enter our minds. If our children perish, it is not God's fault. Many parents do not believe God's promise and follow His Word. Andrew Murray wrote:

> God expects that the children of believers should be believers too. There is nothing so honoring or pleasing to God as believing Him; nothing so opens the way for His blessing and love to flow in and take possession of us than that we believe Him. And the very object and purpose of God in the institution of the parental

covenant is that believing parents should educate believing children. They are the children of the promise;
God and His grace are theirs in promise. A promise
has no value but as it is believed; parents who truly
believe will understand that it is their privilege and
their duty to train "children that believe" (Titus 1:6).
(*How to Raise Your Children for Christ*, 277)

Never think that God doesn't care about your child's eternal destiny. Satan knows that his evil work prospers wherever
such error thrives. If he can somehow preclude the loving
nature of God from shining down into our souls, then perhaps
he can prevent us from believing and claiming the promises of
God for our families.

I remember the transformation that took place in my
own life when I began to trust God's love. The text that God
used was Hebrews 11:6: "And without faith it is impossible to
please Him, for he who comes to God must believe that He
is, and that He is a rewarder of those who seek Him." It was
as if God was saying to me: "When you pray to Me, you *must*
believe that I want to hear you and help you. I am not indifferent to your needs. I love you. I want to give you what you
need. I want to help, to save, to answer. You don't have to
twist My arm or convince Me of your legitimate needs and
desires. Come, and I will reward you. I will answer you in
such a way and at such a time as is best. I am a God of
love."

The person who doubts this should not expect that he will
receive anything from the Lord (James 1:7). Maybe that is why
many of us have never seen God's power unleashed in behalf
of our families. We just don't believe that God is the God of love
He declares Himself to be. We doubt that He really wants to
save our families and bless us. And there may be some who
believe and yet haven't received their answer from God. Hang
on—it will surely come. He will faithfully do as He promised
when it will bring Him the most glory. Answers do not always
come quickly.

The Life of Jesus

Jesus was "the image of the invisible God," as "it was the Father's good pleasure for all the fulness to dwell in Him" (Col. 1:15, 19). When He walked on earth, He could say, "He who has seen me has seen the Father" (John 14:9). To have seen Jesus, then, was to have seen God. To have watched Him live was to have viewed how God wants us to live in this world. The life of Jesus was the clearest revelation of His will that God had ever made. John knew this and declared, "The Word became flesh, and dwelt among us, and we beheld His glory, glory as of the only begotten from the Father, full of grace and truth. . . . No man has seen God at any time; the only begotten God, who is in the bosom of the Father, He has explained Him" (John 1:14, 18).

If God desires the salvation and blessing of believers' children, certainly Jesus would have revealed such in His life and teachings. But did He? Did the Son of God ever signify a special place in His heart for these little ones? If He did, then we have good grounds upon which to build our hopes for their salvation. If He did not, then we seem doomed to uncertainty concerning the welfare of their dear souls. What does the Bible say about the Savior's attitude toward the children of believers?

Isaiah 40:11

> Like a shepherd He will tend His flock, in His arm He
> will gather the lambs, and carry them in His bosom;
> He will gently lead the nursing ewes.

This prophecy of the coming Messiah portrays Him as one who tenderly cares for the whole flock—old and young, male and female. Isaiah gives special notice of the Shepherd's carefully gathering the lambs around Himself, even lifting them up and pressing them into the safety of His own chest. This brief picture also places emphasis on His compassion for young mothers as they care for their young. He will gently lead them, giving them the guidance they need as they nurse and raise these helpless creatures. They want the best for their little ones, and He will not abandon them. He is not insensitive to their maternal wishes.

How was this prophecy fulfilled in the life of Jesus the Messiah? Is it just a spiritual lesson about the general care of Christ for believers, or is there something special here for parents and their children? The Gospel accounts settle these questions for us. Yes, Jesus cares for and loves the children of believers. This wonderful truth is represented in several key passages.

Mark 10:13–16 (cf. Matt. 19:13–15; Luke 18:15–17)

And they were bringing children to Him so that He might touch them; and the disciples rebuked them. But when Jesus saw this, He was indignant and said to them, "Permit the children to come to Me; do not hinder them; for the kingdom of God belongs to such as these. Truly I say to you, whoever does not receive the kingdom of God like a child shall not enter it at all." And He took them in His arms and began blessing them, laying His hands upon them.

This is a remarkable passage. What a revelation of the hearts of men is portrayed in these few lines. Some parents wanted to bring their little children ("babies" in Luke's narrative) to Jesus for a blessing. But the disciples disagreed and even rebuked them for doing so. *The Lord certainly has more important matters to deal with than to concern Himself with children,* they thought. *Indeed! What a waste of His precious time to turn His great mind and poignant speeches away from an enthralled crowd of adults, to deal with the undeveloped minds of children,* they may have reasoned.

When Jesus saw this, He was filled with indignation. The word depicting His outrage is used nowhere else of Him in Scripture. It portrays great anger and is used to describe the emotion of the chief priests when the crowds were shouting to Jesus, "Hosanna to the Son of David" (Matt. 21:15).

Does it surprise you that the sinless Son of God should become so angered by the disciples' hindering little babies from being brought to Him? If it does, the whole point of this book is to convince you that God really does desire to bless the families of believers. Jesus used the occasion to warn His disciples in stern language never to minimize that truth.

He declared that the kingdom of God belongs to little children as well as to adults. Then, doing just what the parents longed for Him to do, Jesus took up their young ones in His arms and blessed them. He actually pronounced a blessing upon these infants. And what do you think of this blessing? Was it a hollow prayer or a token gesture by a professional clergyman? No! He gave them the very blessing of God. And all whom God blesses shall be blessed! No power of man or Satan can thwart the will of God. When Jesus blessed these little ones, they received the certain blessings intended by the Messiah.

What joy must have filled the parents' hearts when Jesus made room for their children! But that was then, and this is now. And the question is, Has He changed since then? Is it His will that parents still seek a blessing from Him for their children? Will He deny to us what He gave to them? Let God's Word supply the answer: "Jesus Christ is the same yesterday and today, yes and forever" (Heb. 13:8). When you come to Him in faith, He will not disappoint you. He stands ready to bless your family too.

Matthew 18:1–6, 10, 14 (cf. Mark 9:33–37; Luke 9:46–48)

At that time the disciples came to Jesus, saying, "Who then is the greatest in the kingdom of heaven?" And He called a child to Himself and set him before them, and said, "Truly I say to you, unless you are converted and become like children, you shall not enter the kingdom of heaven. Whoever then humbles himself as this child, he is the greatest in the kingdom of heaven.

And whoever receives one such child in My name receives Me; but whoever causes one of these little ones who believe in Me to stumble, it is better for him that a heavy millstone be hung around his neck, and that he be drowned in the depth of the sea. . . . See that you do not despise one of these little ones, for I say to you, that their angels in heaven continually behold the face of My Father who is in heaven. . . . Thus it is not the will of your Father who is in heaven that one of these little ones perish."

When Jesus exalts the attribute of childlike humility, He seems to imply that children, more than adults, are good soil for the word of salvation. The Lord also identifies Himself with children in a beautiful way. He tells His disciples that what they do for (or against) such a child, God views as being done to Himself. Yes, God cares deeply for these children. Yet how often are they overlooked by followers of Christ today?

In as serious a warning as Jesus ever gives to His disciples, He admonishes them not to disregard youthful believers. He solemnly states that it would be better to suffer a terrible physical death than to meet the judgment that will surely come on all who cause these children to stumble. Intent on promoting the welfare of children, Jesus urges his disciples to rivet their thoughts on them, instead of just giving them a few fleeting moments of their precious time. He goes so far as to threaten with "fiery hell" those who disregard His words (v. 9).

Jesus intended to make certain that the disciples have a positive attitude toward children, and so he warned them not to "despise one of these little ones" (v. 10). That doesn't leave much room for misunderstanding. Not one of them should be despised or neglected. If the ministries of the church today neglect them, if the preaching of the pulpit overlooks them, if the agendas of adults discount them—these failings must be changed.

When our urban church became convinced that children are Jesus' priority, we looked for ways to minister to them. We added a children's message (five to ten minutes) to our morning worship service. And we began celebrating "Children's Days" every month that had a fifth Sunday. On those Sundays the children took part in many parts of the service. They were greeters and ushers, took up the offering, led in special music, and read the Scripture (older ones), and we crafted the message especially for them. We Christians need to be creative and profuse in ministering to Christ's little lambs.

To add more force to His words, Jesus says that these little ones have angels dispatched by God who are ever ready to assist them. God evidently thinks a lot more of children than we do. And if we resist His care for them, we could find ourselves fighting the very hosts of heaven whom the Lord marshaled for their benefit (cf. Heb. 1:14).

The climax of this whole subject as taught by Jesus is found in verse 14. There the Son of God declared, "It is not the will of your Father who is in heaven that one of these little ones perish." What more needs to be said? God has spoken! He has revealed through the ministry of His holy Son that it is His will to bless believers and their children. He has used solemn and clear language to dissuade anyone from ignoring, overlooking, despising, or neglecting children. He has warned His ministers not to hinder any parent from coming to Him for a blessing on his or her children. And those who have had faith to come, He has rewarded with a divine blessing upon their children because He does not desire that any of them perish.

In fact, some of the most wonderful promises Christ gave to needy souls were in the context of parents' seeking a blessing for their children. A Canaanite mother persistently cried out to the Lord for her demonized daughter. Jesus praised her faith, saying, "Be it done for you as you wish," and her daughter was immediately healed! (Matt. 15:22–28). A father brought his demonized son to Jesus for healing. Jesus declared, "All things are possible to him who believes" (Mark 9:23). After the father humbly admitted his unbelief, saying, "I do believe; help me in my unbelief" (v. 24), his son was delivered on the spot.

A ruler of a synagogue fell at Jesus' feet, begging Him to heal his only child, a twelve-year-old girl. Word arrived that the little girl had died and that he should not "trouble" Jesus anymore (Luke 8:49). The narrative continues, "But when Jesus heard this, He answered him, 'Do not be afraid any longer; only believe, and she shall be made well'"(v. 50). Jesus went to the man's home and healed his daughter.

A royal official caught up to Jesus at Cana and asked Him to heal his sick son in Capernaum. Jesus sent him away, saying, "Go your way; your son lives" (John 4:50). And in Nain the Lord came up alongside a weeping widow as she went out to bury her only son. "He felt compassion for her" (Luke 7:13), told her not to weep, and raised her son from the dead.

What possible sorrow in our lives as parents is not included in these accounts? We see a mother pleading for her daughter, a father for his son, a father for his daughter, a widow for her son. The children are dead, diseased, demonized—and what does Jesus say? Do not weep! Do not be afraid! *Only believe!*

The same words go forth today. Who can say to parents today that Jesus does not want to help their child? Christ does not demand perfect faith. Admit your unbelief and ask him to help you. He hasn't changed. He is God, and God cannot change! Cast away your unbelief and claim His mercy for your children.

We have found in the love of God and in the life of Christ unquestionable evidence of God's desire to save believers and their families. (For more biblical evidence of God's promises to the family, see Appendix A.) Do not let anything keep you from believing and acting on the Word of God. Make the promises of God the convictions of your entire life. Do not abandon them when faced with difficulties and trials. Like Victoria, claim the promises of God through prayer when all else seems lost. You will find God to be faithful to all who sacrifice for the sake of their children. Our sons' and daughters' souls have been entrusted to our care. Will we love them as God does and claim the promises He has given us for their salvation?

Discussion Questions

1. How does the love of God reveal His desire to save the children of believers?

2. In what ways has Satan tempted you to doubt the love of God?

3. Why is it impossible to love and honor God without loving and honoring Jesus?

4. Why do you think Jesus became so angry at His disciples for discouraging the parents who were seeking His blessing on their children?

5. In what ways do we as individuals and as churches cause little ones to stumble? What should we do to remedy this problem?

6. Do you really believe that what you do for or against God's little believers is viewed by God as done to Himself? How will this affect your relationship to your own children?

7. What remark by Jesus concerning children most affected you? Why?

8. Which instance of a Christ-seeking parent in the Gospels most impacted you? Why?

❖ PART THREE ❖

Our Duty

❖ Chapter Six ❖

The Instruction of Parents

Life is full of agreements. Some are formal, like securing a bank loan to buy a car. If the borrower does not keep up the monthly payments, the car is repossessed; the contract is broken and the borrower no longer enjoys the promise of using and owning the car. Most agreements are informal. Informal agreements also have consequences when they are broken. If one promises to meet a person and discuss a matter with him, there are consequences for not showing up. If there is no good excuse, there will be a loss of trust in the one who has broken the appointment. Life teaches us that irresponsibility bears negative results. The subject of parental responsibility is no different.

A Contract with God

Every believing parent is in a type of partnership with God. Like other formal agreements or contracts, the one we have with God includes both responsibilities and consequences. As I mentioned in the preface, this agreement is conditional; there are conditions that parents are to fulfill if they want to receive the promises. If we do what we are supposed to do, then God will do as He has promised in blessing us. If we discard the contract, there will be negative consequences.

Some of God's promises are unconditional. They speak of things that He has said He would do regardless of the actions of others. He said He would send His Son to bring salvation, He would raise the dead, He would make a new heaven and earth. Many other promises of God are conditional, like the family promises we are discussing, the fulfillment of which hinges on the response of parents. As the originator of the contract with families, it is God, not we, who has designed its terms. He has essentially said, "If you believe and obey, then I will bless your home." He usually fulfills that promise soon, but there are times when He waits until later. When God waits, His glory and our good are always in view. He is a loving and good God who does nothing unwisely or malevolently.

What a solemn thing this covenant is! God has graciously made a promise that He will bring salvation to the families of faithful believers. Thus far we have attempted to prove that God has made promises to parents for their families. Having done that, we will begin in this chapter to see what the responsibilities of the parents are in this partnership.

Faith—the Ultimate Condition

The Lord told Abraham, our spiritual father:"I am God Almighty; walk before Me, and be blameless. And I will establish My covenant between Me and you" (Gen. 17:1–2). The covenant would not be fulfilled unless Abraham kept his part. But, you may be wondering, who can be blameless? None of us can be blameless in ourselves. However, we can all become blameless by faith in Jesus Christ. Though none of us can perfectly perform our duties, God accepts our imperfect obedience when its comes from a sincere heart moved by faith in His Son.

Abraham trusted that the Messiah would come and bear the guilt for his sins (John 8:56). He was saved by his faith (Heb. 11:13). And his family was blessed for it.

Abraham was imperfect in his obedience. He grievously sinned in Gerar and jeopardized the purity of his wife, Sarah (Gen. 20:1–18). Nevertheless, God forgave his sin and accepted Abraham as righteous. For this reason, the Lord said to Abraham's son, Isaac, "I will multiply your descendants as the stars of heaven, and will give your descendants all these lands; and by your descendants all the nations of the earth shall by blessed; *because Abraham obeyed me, and kept My charge, My commandments, My statutes and My laws*" (Gen. 26:4–5). But did Abraham obey perfectly? No. Was he blameless in all he did? Of course not. His *faith* "was reckoned to him as righteousness" (Rom. 4:3). And Isaac was blessed after him.

We as parents will not perfectly keep our part of the covenant, but our faith in Christ can make up the difference. God expects us to try our best. But while Christ's righteousness does not give us freedom to sin without consequences (Rom. 6:1–2), His righteousness does assure us that all that we do by faith for His glory and honor will be accepted by the Father through Him. Every duty done for our children in Christ's name is a sweet aroma to the Father.

God also made a similar promise to David, saying, "If your sons will keep My covenant, and My testimony which I will teach them, *their sons shall sit upon your throne forever*" (Ps. 132:12). Here again we have an agreement made by God. It demanded obedience from David's sons. If they obeyed, God would bless their sons. If they did not believe and obey, the covenant would no longer be binding. This particular covenant was broken by David's sons and never realized.

God has made wonderful promises to parents concerning their children, but parents must remember that these promises are conditional. Some are realized and others are not. Parents must have Christ-centered faith and Bible-centered obedience if they wish to receive God's blessings on their families. How do we come to possess these essential qualities? The source is God, so that there is no place for human pride. All parental success is by grace. The faith and obedience we need are His gifts to us.

Requirements of God's Family Contract

It is time to examine what God requires of parents in His agreement with them for their families. What are the biblical commands that parents are to obey? I pray that God will give you determination and faith as you read them: determination to do your duty in your home, and faith, like Abraham's, to believe that it is not merely your own imperfect obedience that will bless your children. The promises are yours *in Christ*. Your faith in Christ covers your imperfection in God's sight. God accepts what you do because you are united with Jesus in doing it. So all of God's promises to His children, including those for our families, are ours to claim through Jesus (2 Cor. 1:20). What then are God's requirements?

Proverbs 22:6

Solomon wrote, "Train up a child in the way he should go, even when he is old he will not depart from it." In this verse we find a duty—"Train up a child in the way he should go"—and a promise—"Even when he is old he will not depart from it." Proverbs 22:6 has been a tremendous blessing and warning to parents for nearly three thousand years. It summarizes the agreement between God and parents in a concise and understandable way. Our children need not go astray, even when they are older and away from our direct oversight.

Think of Daniel and his three friends. They were taken away from their parents and tempted with the lifestyle of a pagan king's court. Yet they remained true to God and their training! Parents can be certain that if they are faithful in raising their children in the way of truth and by the grace of God, then the Lord will faithfully keep their children in the way of righteousness. What a promise! We can be the actual vessels through which spiritual and physical blessings are communicated to our children if we do our part. If however we do not do our part, we break the agreement and should not be surprised if our families are devoured by sin and sadness.

The responsibility summarized so beautifully in Proverbs 22:6 is carefully explained in detail elsewhere in the Word of God. What are the duties of parents in relationship to their children? What is involved in "training up a child in the way he should go"? Scripture spells out four basic areas of responsibility demanded of parents as their part in the wonderful family covenant that God has made. We will look at the first one in this chapter and the remaining three in the following three chapters.

Instruction

The Lord has often commanded parents to teach their children the Word of God. The way of God's Word is "the way they should go." So if parents faithfully teach the Bible to their children *and do not neglect the other duties,* they can be assured that the Lord will deal mercifully with their children.

Deuteronomy 4:9–10 and 6:5–7

The Lord used the following words of Moses to amplify the importance of biblical instruction:

> Give heed to yourself and keep your soul diligently, lest you forget the things which your eyes have seen, and lest they depart from your heart all the days of your life; but *make them known to your sons and grandsons.* Remember the day you stood before the LORD your God at Horeb, when the LORD said to me, "Assemble the people to Me, that I may let them hear My words so they may learn to fear Me all the days they live on the earth, and that they may *teach their children.*" (Deut. 4:9–10)

And you shall love the LORD your God with all your
heart and with all your soul and with all your might.
And these words, which I am commanding you today,
shall be on your heart; and you shall *teach them diligently to your sons* and shall talk of them when you sit in
your house and when you walk by the way and when
you lie down and when you rise up. (Deut. 6:5–7; cf.
11:19)

Two things especially warrant our reflection in these passages. First, parents are commanded to teach *what was in their
own hearts*. In other words, our instruction should be red-hot off
the burning altars of our own souls, rather than cold and
formal. I have been deeply impressed by passionate teaching in
the past. I remember my mother often weeping as she taught
us God's Word. She was passing on to her sons what she
sincerely believed, not simply some interesting lesson. She would
sometimes pray that God would give her sons what she called
"the gift of tears." I don't know where she got that phrase, but
she knew that her sons needed soft, pliable hearts that deeply
and evidently appreciated God's Word and reflected His mercy, and souls that could cry for joy and for grief.

Many parents fail in this regard. They have no passion for
God. They don't manifest a love for the Word of God. Kids can
easily tell when parents are just "doing their duty." Our teaching should be compelling. But in order for it to move others, it
must first move us. The truth must first be "on our hearts" if we
want our children to embrace it.

Second, the two texts from Deuteronomy emphasize that
biblical instruction be the central theme in the home. "These
words" (the commands of Scripture) are to permeate every
aspect of life at every moment. Is that true of your home?

We parents should use the Bible to interact with everything in life, both the positive and the negative, in training our
children. As I seek God's wisdom to do this daily, I am learning
to teach my kids through everything we encounter. That ability
does not come easily. All of us have to start where we are, like

babies learning to walk. The more we practice, the better skilled we become. For example, think of today's news headlines and ask yourself, What truth in God's Word does this teach? Does it show that "the wages of sin is death" (Rom. 6:23)? Perhaps it reveals that the heart is deceitful and desperately sick (Jer. 17:9). Think the question through and discuss it with your family. This is how you lay the foundation of knowledge—stone by stone.

Many of us parents do not think enough about the world around us and see how it glorifies God (Ps. 19:1). So how can we show our children that the world is in God's control? To do that we need to focus our thoughts on God, which at first can require more mental effort than you realize. Ask God to help you. Take little steps and begin today. Develop the habit of turning everything Godward in the home. When that happens, everyone learns to take part and can glorify God through all the various events of life. We have found that our children enjoy talking about the Bible's relevance to life while we're in the car, around the table, or just about anywhere.

If we don't teach our children, someone else will. Kids will learn because their minds long for knowledge. If they are being chiefly influenced by their friends, televisions, radios, magazines, or comic books, we are failing. If we are not carefully monitoring what our children are being taught through these sources, *we are not keeping our part of the agreement with God,* which demands constant Bible-centered instruction. These commands given through Moses were not only for the Israelites. They are for us, too.

How does our responsibility for our children's instruction relate to their formal schooling, particularly if the government forbids teaching the Bible in school? Many Christian parents have come to the conviction that they cannot entrust their children to the public school system as it presently operates. That decision brings on them tremendous financial pressure, to be sure. But what is the alternative? To allow their children to spend thirteen hundred hours per year under the authority of Bible-rejecting mentors? For many of us, that is no true alternative.

My wife and I have decided that we will sacrifice all that needs to be sacrificed in order to ensure that our children are taught God's Word throughout the day and in all areas of their education. I thank God that Christian schools and the home school movement make such an education possible for many of us. But what about other parents? We should do what we can to assist our brothers and sisters who desire to educate their children biblically but are financially unable. There are many for whom neither Christian schooling nor home schooling is a viable option. The church must labor and sacrifice in order to help these members instruct their covenant children.

While I was pastoring an inner-city church, we established a fund to help parents who could not otherwise afford Christian education for their children. In some cases the church helped pay for tuition at a Christian school. In others, we helped to purchase home school materials. We were a far-from-wealthy church, but we prayed that the Lord would provide and saw Him do so in some amazing ways. Older Christians or those with more resources can "adopt" young people by helping to meet the costs of their Christian education. The little lambs in other Christian families are partly our responsibility too. If we call ourselves one family, one flock, it would only seem right that we function that way.

Psalm 78:1–8 and 2 Timothy 3:14–15

Listen, O my people, to my instruction. . . . I will utter dark sayings of old, which we have heard and known, and our fathers have told us. *We will not conceal them from their children, but tell to the generation to come* the praises of the LORD, and His strength and His wondrous works that He has done. For He established a testimony in Jacob, and appointed a law in Israel, which He commanded our fathers, *that they should teach them to their children*, that the generation to come might know, even the children yet to be born, that they may arise and tell them to their children, that they should put their confidence in God, and not forget the works of God, but keep His commandments, and not be like their fathers, a stubborn and rebellious generation, a generation that did not prepare its heart, and whose spirit was not faithful to God. (Ps. 78:1–8)

You, however, continue in the things you have learned and become convinced of, knowing from whom you have learned them; and that from childhood you have known the sacred writings which are able to give you the wisdom that leads to salvation through faith which is in Christ Jesus. (2 Tim. 3:14–15)

In these texts the Lord states that parents' teaching of the Word normally leads to their children's salvation. There is a God-given connection between our instructing our children and their salvation. In another text, the prophet Joel said, "Tell your sons . . . and let your sons tell their sons, and their sons the next generation" (Joel 1:3). The implication is that, as the Word of the Lord is faithfully taught in the home, each generation receives it in faith and passes it on to the next. Clearly, the home is to be built on the Bible. Every event of life should be related to the testimony of God, and every question should be answered by referring to the Word. In this way our children learn that God is both trustworthy and in control. He does as He says.

How is the Enemy destroying our homes? The way is evident—through *insufficient Bible teaching*. God said: "My people are destroyed for lack of knowledge. Because you have rejected knowledge, I also will reject you. . . . Since you have forgotten the law of your God, *I also will forget your children*" (Hos. 4:6).

Parents that do not have regular times of Bible study with their children are dooming their homes. Parents that go day after day without raising spiritual themes for discussion with their children are rebelling against God and forsaking their duty. There must be no vacation from Christian education in the home! You are to teach your children "when you sit in your house and when you walk by the way and when you lie down and when you rise up" (Deut. 6:7).

We need to repent of the sin of not rightly instructing our children. The blood of these precious ones will be on our hands if we do not repent and "bring forth fruit in keeping with repentance" (Matt. 3:8). Where there is repentance there is hope. We are not abandoned to guilt and failure. And so, dear friend, always look to Jesus. He died for our sins and can help us to replace the old ways of sin with the new ways of righteousness. None of us can perfectly instruct our children. But our sincere attempt to train them, depending on Jesus to give them saving grace, will surely be blessed by the One who said, "Thus it is not the will of your Father who is in heaven that one of these little ones perish" (Matt. 18:14).

Long ago, a preacher wrote:

> I shall close up this with one word to those who are parents. Consider what a great charge God hath instructed you with. In your hands are deposited the hope and blessing, or else the curse and plague, of the next age. Your families are nurseries both of Church and State; and according to the cultivating of them now, such will their fruits be hereafter. (Hopkins, *The Works of Ezekiel Hopkins*, 1:402)

I know of a young boy who was institutionalized because his parents divorced and could not take care of him. He was growing very bitter and getting into a lot of trouble. His father's brother, already with several children of his own, took on the responsibility of raising this young boy. The troubled boy was thus brought into a Christian home and loved as a son. For years he was instructed in the Bible, both at home and in his formal schooling. There were some tough times to be sure, but the uncle and aunt persevered in giving their nephew the atmosphere of a Christian home in which to grow up.

Today, he is a young man with a Christian wife and two

beautiful children. He and his wife both teach in a Christian school and are raising their children according to God's family promises. He is also enjoying a growing relationship with his own father, too. These lives and relationships were eternally changed because a couple loved someone else's child as their own and were willing to sacrifice to help him. By God's grace this boy received the instruction of the Lord and, with it, a knowledge of salvation, which he now passes on to others.

Discussion Questions

1. What was Abraham's duty in his agreement with God? Did he fulfill his duty? How?
2. Discuss the duty and promise included in Proverbs 22:6.
3. Discuss the implications of obeying Deuteronomy 6:7 today.
4. How seriously have you taken your duty of providing Christian education for your children in your home? In their formal education?
5. What texts show that the Lord often uses parents' teaching to save their children? Has this been so with your children? Discuss.
6. What are the chief obstacles in your home that hinder the biblical instruction of your children? How can these best be removed?

Chapter Seven

The Discipline of Parents

My son asked my wife if he could go to the mall and hang out with friends from his Christian school. My kids, like yours, know which parent to go to when they want something specific. Debby and I both have our own areas of weakness, which the kids are prone to exploit. And so, we find safety in consulting with each other when they ask for certain things. In this case, Debby didn't think it was a good idea for John to go. After giving it some thought, I agreed with her. So we sat down with John and explained to him why we didn't think his going to the mall unsupervised was in his best interests.

I shared with him some thoughts about Satan's schemes (2 Cor. 2:11), the power of evil, and the nearly irresistible force of peer pressure over a person's character. We also talked about the many anti-Christian influences in the mall's arcade, the kids' gathering place. We offered him some alternative choices, such as inviting a friend or two over to our house. Although John wasn't delighted with the outcome, he abided by it. Little did we know how powerfully the Lord would reinforce the wisdom of our decision.

Not long thereafter, a story filled the news media about the brutal beating death of a Philadelphia youth. He was killed by a group of teenagers from our area who had been provoked by an incident involving the slain boy. Misinformation had spread, stirring fires of anger, and a few kids became bent on a fight. The night ended with one boy being beaten to death with a bat. No one had expected things to go as far as they did, but no one ever does.

The details of that night's events deeply impressed my son and confirmed our counsel. A couple of angered kids had gotten into a car and headed to the mall in search of peers who would join them in the confrontation. It was the same mall that my son wanted to visit. Two carloads of excited kids soon gathered, and they left looking for trouble. They were going to teach the kids from the other neighborhood a lesson.

The eyewitness accounts were shocking. One after another the boys took turns pulverizing their victim. They seemed to be out of their minds, inciting each other to greater and greater acts of brutality. After a couple of weeks of investigation, seven boys were charged with murder. Young boys, several of whom went to the mall just to hang out with friends, had ruined their lives—and destroyed another's life.

The point of this story is not that going to the mall is bad or that my son or yours would kill someone. But Satan does seek to defile and destroy our children (1 Peter 5:8), and he is more likely to do that when kids are unsupervised, when their guards are down, and when they are most vulnerable to peer pressure. I am sure that the parents of the seven boys charged with murder wished their sons had not gone to the mall that night. Our not allowing John to go was a small act of discipline. Discipline sets boundaries, explains them, and enforces them, and so that is what we did in his best interests. We did so because we were convinced that he, like all kids, needs loving discipline.

Much Given, Much Required

The Lord deals with His people as a wise ruler or landlord deals with those under him (see Matt. 25:14–30; Luke 19:11–27). He gives to each of us certain gifts and opportunities and expects a fair return on His investment. His policy is, "From everyone who has been given much shall much be required" (Luke 12:48). By giving us families, the Lord has entrusted "much" to us parents. He has made great promises concerning what He will do through us and for us. But He has never promised to bless our families automatically. He expects us to do our part.

Grace to Do Our Part

It is God who graciously enables us to fulfill our responsibilities, if we ask Him to. That was true of Abraham, of whom the Lord said, "I have chosen him, in order that he may command his children and his household after him to keep the way of the LORD by doing righteousness and justice; in order that the LORD may bring upon Abraham what He has spoken about him" (Gen. 18:19). What a wonderful statement of God's grace and human responsibility! God chose Abraham by grace. Abraham then commanded and led his family in such a way that he received the promises of God. That too was by God's grace, but it required Abraham's most determined efforts.

Like Abraham, we are in a sacred agreement with God. We saw in chapter 6 that He expects and commands us to instruct our children in the Word of God. As we consider now our responsibility to discipline our children, we must not forget that we sinners have no hope of doing our duty except by His empowering grace. But we *can* face our duties with confidence that God will supply the grace we need. He is, after all, "the God of all grace" (1 Peter 5:10). His majestic and exalted throne is called "the throne of grace," so that we need never hesitate to approach Him with any need. Paul encourages us to seek grace from Him because "God is able to make all grace abound to you, that always having all sufficiency in everything, you may have an abundance for every good deed" (2 Cor. 9:8).

So as we proceed to examine other parental duties in this and the next two chapters, let us understand that God *will* give us what we need and ask for in behalf of His precious children. "Let us therefore draw near with confidence to the throne of grace, that we may receive mercy and may find grace to help in time of need" (Heb. 4:16).

Delivering Children from Destruction

Consistent, loving discipline will have eternal consequences for your children. Solomon wrote: "Do not hold back discipline from the child, although you beat him with the rod, he will not die. You shall beat him with the rod, and deliver his soul from Sheol" (Prov. 23:13–14).

Why does God associate discipline with delivering a child from destruction? Let me suggest an answer: Before a child can be useful to God or society, he or she must understand that sin causes sadness. Children must learn that they *never* benefit from sinning, however beneficial it may seem at the moment. Because God rules all things, we have the assurance that His justice and truth shall eventually prevail. The Lord states that "the wages of sin is death" (Rom. 6:23). If we allow our children to sin without temporal consequences, then we are teaching them a horrible lie. Our permissiveness conveys to them that sin does not bring sadness and destruction. And what they learn in the home, they usually carry throughout life. If they have "gotten away with murder" as children, they will likely attempt to do the same as adults.

The reverse is equally true. Just as sin causes inevitable sadness, holiness and obedience bring happiness. As parents, we ought to reward our children for their obedience, thereby forming within their impressionable souls the vital link between happiness and holiness. In this way a parent prepares a child well for both a relationship with God and a productive role in society.

Examples of Parental Neglect

God's Word records many sad instances of parental neglect of discipline. Consider carefully the example of Eli:

> And the LORD said to Samuel, "Behold, I am about to do a thing in Israel at which both ears of everyone who hears it will tingle. In that day I will carry out against Eli all that I have spoken concerning his house, from beginning to end. For I have told him that I am about to judge his house forever for the iniquity which he knew, *because his sons brought a curse on themselves and he did not rebuke them.* And therefore I have sworn to the house of Eli that the iniquity of Eli's house shall not be atoned for by sacrifice or offering forever." (1 Sam. 3:11–14)

Eli had known about his sons' sin and had admonished them for it (1 Sam. 2:22–24). But that apparently was as far as he went. He did not put any bite into his words. His sons had not learned to associate sin with its consequences. God, therefore, accused Eli of honoring his sons more than he honored God (v. 29), and He promised to bring serious judgment on his house. God warned, "Those who honor Me I will honor, and those who despise Me will be lightly esteemed" (v. 30). When a parent chooses not to discipline his child for sin, he dishonors and despises God, and he shall be "lightly esteemed" by God if the trend continues.

I am sure that Eli's permissiveness started long before this judgment was pronounced. Early in their lives children express a rebellious will by challenging their parents. Some parents laugh it off, saying, "Isn't that cute; such a naughty boy!" and the pattern goes on for weeks and months. Before long the tantrums begin. Parents who don't understand that the child is actually challenging their authority foolishly give the child whatever he demands, thereby setting a deadly precedent. The child quickly learns that he can win. He has faced the will of the parent and has prevailed. Though these may not be his conscious thoughts, they form an unmistakable expectation—a habit—leading to further selfishness, sorrow, and rebellion. Through trial and error, a child figures out just how far he can go without being punished. He pushes the limits time and time again, stretching the bounds of his parents' rules. Some parents continue to give in until there are no boundaries left, and they have lost all respect in their child's eyes.

Something like that appears to have happened in the life of Samson. He was a gift from God and blessed by the Lord (Judg. 13:3, 24). But somewhere along the line, Manoah and his wife began to concede to the demands of their son. Eventually things reached the point where Samson insisted that his father arrange for him to marry a Philistine because she looked good to him (Judg. 14:3). Though his parents protested, they had lost influence and honor in Samson's eyes. His several illicit relationships with women blemished his life and usefulness to the Lord from then on. Although in the end God revived him, it was not before he had been blinded, imprisoned, and humiliated.

To Spank or Not to Spank?

God has prescribed discipline as an effective antidote to the spread of evil in a child's life. The form of discipline, though often physical, may vary. Solomon said, "The *rod* and *reproof* give wisdom, but a child who gets his own way brings shame to his mother" (Prov. 29:15).

The purpose of the rod is to impress upon a child the connection between sin and pain. Verbal reproof is also an effective tool. Some children may rarely need physical discipline; words of rebuke always humble them, bringing them to repentance. Others need to feel the physical pain; they just do not learn by verbal reproof alone. Reproof involving the temporary retraction of a child's privileges is also an effective form of discipline. Kids often learn more by missing out on something they like than by feeling physical pain. We need to ask

God for wisdom to discern which form of discipline is most appropriate for each child in each situation. Older children, for example, are better disciplined by reproof or loss of freedoms than by the rod. But if they have been allowed to sin without consequence during their earlier years, discipline by any means will not likely prove as effective when they become teenagers.

The Manner of Discipline

The effectiveness of discipline is often determined by how it is administered. All discipline should be fair and consistent. Make sure you have the facts straight before disciplining your child. Anger can short-circuit this process and cause parents to react hastily before they have the whole story. Discipline out of love, not out of anger. In this way you will imitate your heavenly Father, "For those whom the LORD loves He disciplines, and He scourges every son whom He receives" (Heb. 12:6). If love is our chief motivation, we need not resort to outbursts of anger or impatience. When we do lose self-control in disciplining a child, we should readily confess that to him or her.

Loving discipline is, nonetheless, firm. Don't be afraid to draw the line for your children. They want you to. I was once told of a girl who tested her mother repeatedly, and after her mother consistently withstood her, the girl thanked her mother for not giving in to her wishes. Yes, children want clear boundaries. Make sure, however, that those boundaries are based on the Scriptures. Let your child know that Jesus wants it this way—and then read the supporting Scripture to him. Your child will gain confidence in your leadership as he sees that you are truly following Jesus.

My wife and I have often been amazed at the effectiveness of prompt, loving discipline. Our children have even come to us at times and asked for it when they have done wrong. They have grown to trust us regarding discipline. This trust did not come easily. Sometimes, having disciplined them out of rash anger, I have gone to them and asked for forgiveness. Had I not humbled myself for my sin of excessive or reckless chastening, would my children have learned to trust me? I doubt they would have.

Many parents have a hard time telling their children that they are sorry, or that they have made a mistake. Such pride is a horrible thing! Our children certainly know we are not perfect, and they do not expect us to be. But they do expect us to be as honest as we want them to be. And when we make a mistake, they love to have us say that we're sorry just as we love to hear them admit when they have done wrong.

Not Neglecting Correction

As we noted earlier, neglecting discipline can have grave consequences. Our willingness to discipline our children is a significant measure of our love for them. "He who spares his rod *hates* his son, but he who *loves* him disciplines him diligently" (Prov. 13:24). Therefore, "Discipline your son while there is hope, and do not desire his *death*" (Prov. 19:18).

That is strong language. To neglect discipline is like seeking the death of your child! He will likely meet destruction because he has never learned to submit his will to those over him. If he does not learn to fear and obey his earthly parents, whom he can see, how is he going to fear and obey God, whom he cannot see? In this very important respect, parents represent God to the young children. By teaching their children to obey (or disobey) human authority, parents are teaching them to honor (or dishonor) the highest authority—God Himself.

That is all the more reason why children need deliberate, systematic correction. It is a horrible blunder to think that things will get better with your children by themselves, given enough time and space. That is the Enemy's lie. Problems of character do not resolve themselves. Things will surely get worse without correction. Children do not mature automatically. What they will become is an extension of what they are today. So do not avoid discipline because it is hard or painful. In the future, both you and the child may sorely regret any lack of the discipline that he or she should have received in childhood. But God's Word offers great hope to conscientious parents: "Correct your son, and he will give you comfort; he will also delight your soul" (Prov. 29:17).

We all fail at times, either by wrongly administering discipline or by not disciplining when we should. But remember that Jesus never fails and that you are accepted in Him. The promises regarding your children are yours ultimately because of His perfect faithfulness, not because of your imperfect faithfulness. "For all the promises of God in Him [Christ] are Yes, and in Him Amen, to the glory of God through us" (2 Cor. 1:20, NKJV).

In addition to all the other wise things Solomon said in the Proverbs, he observed that "foolishness is bound up in the heart of a child; the rod of discipline will remove it far from him" (Prov. 22:15). In Old Testament terminology, the fool was an unbeliever and the wise were believers. The foolishness bound up in a child's heart, of which Solomon spoke, is not simply horseplay and childishness. It is the seed of selfishness and ungodliness deeply sown within each human child. But thank God that discipline is one of the ways that He has chosen to remove it from your child and lead him or her to salvation.

Discussion Questions

1. Why is it wrong to think that God is going to automatically bless us and our families? How do you think that notion came to be embraced by so many people today?
2. What are the four duties parents are to perform in their part of God's family covenant?
3. How does physical discipline affect a child's spiritual destiny?
4. What are the two main forms of discipline that Solomon mentions in Proverbs 29:15? When is one form more suitable than the other form?
5. Why, in your opinion, do so many people today oppose physical discipline for their families?

❖ CHAPTER EIGHT ❖

The Example of Parents

A good role model is one of the most powerful influences on earth.

I will never forget watching the evening news one night and being overcome with emotion at the closing story, about a simple southern gentleman. I cannot remember his name, but that isn't important. It was not *who* he was that amazed me but *what* he was. Though he lived in what many of us would consider poverty, he possessed a wealth that could not be measured in dollars and a power that few of us will ever realize. He was indeed a rare individual, which is why NBC ran his story.

The story centered on his daily routine. Following a busy day at work, he would visit elderly folk, widows, and single mothers all over town, regardless of race. Stopping at home after home, he would ask how he could help. If there was something to be fixed, he would fix it. If someone needed groceries for supper, he would go out and buy them—at his own expense. If someone just needed to talk, he would stop and listen, offering sympathy or humble advice fitting at the moment. And he did it all in the name of Jesus—rejoicing! It was no burden to him, no duty that he reluctantly fulfilled once a month. This was his life, what he chose to do with his time, energy, and money.

When that short piece was over, I sensed that I had witnessed a truly great man. I was moved by the power of his loving service, and I found myself wanting to be like him.

People who are good examples have a way of drawing others to imitate them. How many young people have been inspired to become missionaries by reading the biographies of legendary missionaries such as David Brainerd, John Eliot, Mary Slessor, John Paton, Henry Martyn, and Hudson Taylor? Their love for Jesus and sacrifice for the gospel are compelling examples, inviting others to follow.

Unfortunately, not all role models influence young people for such noble ends. From relativistic school teachers and materialistic peers to promiscuous entertainers and corrupt public officials, there are more than enough evil examples competing for children's attention. In the face of so many bad influences, a child desperately needs good, consistent examples worth following. And no one is in a better position to provide them than a child's own parents in the home.

Few parents appreciate the importance of their own example in the lives of their kids. Whether moms and dads realize it or not, they have an immense impact on their children—for good or evil—by the example they set. Good parenting does not stop with teaching and correcting their sons and daughters. As important as instruction and discipline are, without the other two parental duties—setting a good example and prayer—all their worthy intentions and positive influence can be nullified. And the alternative to a good example is not *no* example, but a *bad* example.

"Like Father, Like Son"

We have all heard the proverb "Like father, like son." A child personifies the qualities modeled by his parents. He becomes what he observes in them. If his parents are hypocrites, he tends to become a hypocrite. If his parents demand more of him than they demand of themselves, he is likely to do the same with his peers. If he is abused as a child, he will more likely abuse his children unless God's grace powerfully intervenes. If his father runs with women, so will he most likely. If a mother neglects her children, her daughters will probably neglect theirs too.

But thank God the opposite is also true. If parents serve the Lord sincerely and consistently in their homes, their children will learn to do the same. If a father exemplifies love and fairness, his sons will also manifest such qualities. If a mother lives a life of modesty and godly submission, so will her daughters. These things, of course, do not happen automatically. A parent cannot be a truly good example while neglecting the other areas of responsibility we have been talking about: instruction, discipline, and prayer. But we must never forget that our example is one of the most powerful influences there is on our children's lives. That should lead each of us to ask, "What kind of model am I to my children? What are they becoming by my example today?"

Family Ties and Tensions

The home is usually united either in obedience or in disobedience. Consider Jeremiah's description of a home united in idolatry: "The *children* gather wood, and the *fathers* kindle the fire, and the *women* knead dough to make cakes for the queen of heaven; and they pour out libations to other gods in order to spite Me" (Jer. 7:18). The fact is that children normally follow their parents' examples. Ungodliness breeds further ungodliness, unless the Lord graciously intervenes.

There are, however, significant exceptions to the norm. Families may be divided in faith. Sometimes true faith resides alongside sheer unbelief in the same household. This condition usually has one of four causes.

1. *A parent becomes saved later in life.* Since he or she did not care about God or His promises earlier in life, the children have learned to follow their natural, sinful inclinations. Unless they come to share their parents' new-found love for Jesus, they will tend not to follow a Christian example.

2. *Christian parents have simply failed to raise their children in the biblical manner.* If, for whatever reason, believers have neglected their parental responsibilities, they have essentially rejected God's covenant concerning their families. It should come as no surprise that their children want no part of Christ.

3. *A Christian marries outside the faith.* Some believers sadly delude themselves into thinking that they can marry an unbeliever and make it work. Paul forbids such marriages, saying that Christians should marry "only in the Lord" (1 Cor. 7:39; cf. 2 Cor. 6:14). Solomon's life was ruined as "his wives turned his heart away after other gods" (1 Kings 11:4). David's heart may have been right with God, but in taking numerous wives he was a bad example for his son Solomon and contributed to his downfall. Homes built on a foundation of spiritual incompatibility very often produce unbelieving children.

I don't want to discourage believing parents who find themselves in such relationships. They still have the promises. Our past unfaithfulness does not void the promises of God if we repent and take up our duties in His strength. We are all unfaithful to some degree. Although we have all failed in many ways, our hope for our children has never been based on our flawless record. Our hope is in Christ. And all the promises to us for our children are to be received by faith in His perfect obedience.

4. *The Lord sometimes sees fit to save the children of faithful parents later in life.* In some families one child may be saved long after the others. Until then, he or she will be at odds with the convictions and example of believing family members.

These exceptions, however, do not disprove the rule that

families are usually united in either truth or error, righteousness or unrighteousness. That unity may not be a peaceful,
harmonious, stable one, particularly when families are entan-
gled in unrighteousness. But even families wracked by strife
usually exhibit common desires, habits, and assumptions—however sinful—which are passed on from one generation to another. Time after time we see children following their parents'
sinful ways. For example:

> Ahaziah the son of Ahab became king over Israel in
> Samaria. . . . And he did evil in the sight of the LORD
> and walked in the way of his father and in the way of
> his mother. . . . So he served Baal and worshiped him
> and provoked the LORD God of Israel to anger accord-
> ing to all that his father had done. (1 Kings 22:51–53)

As a current example, a large percentage of men now in
jail have or had fathers who also served time. Though these
fathers may not have intended to teach their sons to break the
law, their sons learned lawlessness simply by being like Dad.

The encouraging thing is that children can learn holiness
by watching their parents, as well. Parents who are good examples can have the joy of seeing their children grow up and
follow their ways. But, again, each of us must ask the question,
"What will my children learn and what will they become by
following my example?"

Modeling Genuine Devotion

Moses said, "Assemble the people, the men and the women and
children . . . in order that they may hear and learn and fear the
LORD your God, *and be careful to observe all the words of this law.*
And their children, who have not known, will hear and learn to
fear the LORD your God" (Deut. 31:12–13). Both parent and
child are commanded to obey God's law. As parents learn to
"observe all the words of [God's] law," their children will in turn

hear and learn to fear the Lord—and, like their parents, *obey*. If parents are "doers of the word, and not merely hearers who delude themselves" (James 1:22), their son and daughters will be spared from self-delusion also.

Parents cannot expect the Word to take hold in their kids if it has not gripped their own lives. What good is it to send children to church and not go with them? How successful is having family devotions when the parents' hearts are not in it? You cannot train a child to be what you are not! There are no short cuts. Giving thanks before meals is no magic potion that will bring God's blessing upon your home. The only way you can keep your part in the agreement with God is *by loving Him with all your heart*. And you can't fake love!

Do your children know that you love Jesus Christ? If you do not love Him, they probably will not love Him either. The Lord regards heart-felt love for God and others to be the most important component of the Christian life—the summation of God's expectations for us (Matt. 22:36–40). Paul concurs in Romans 13:8–10 and 1 Corinthians 13. Without genuine love, all our words and external motions ring hollow to our children.

I was deeply impressed by my parents' unmistakable love for Jesus. I saw them make decisions involving tremendous personal sacrifice out of love for Christ and others. I heard them boldly witness about Him to everyone. And I want my children to know how much I love Jesus, too. I purposely talk about Him and openly associate with Him. I eagerly talk of Him and walk with Him in my everyday contacts with unbelievers and believers alike.

Love of God is what makes teaching about God effective. Moses expressed the order of priorities this way: "You shall love the LORD your God with all your heart and with all your soul and with all your might. And these words, which I am commanding you today, shall be on your heart; and you shall teach them diligently to your sons" (Deut. 6:5–7). It is fruitless to instruct your children in the Bible if you yourself do not love the central figure of the Bible. Children will see the shallowness of your teaching and will likely dismiss it as false or irrelevant.

If it isn't important enough to affect the way you live, they will hardly think it crucial for their lives either.

Dad and Mom, is Jesus a real person to you? Is He with you now? Is His presence the most important thing in your life? Do you order your day, your thoughts, your plans with His pleasure in mind? Is Jesus your King? Do you love Him? Does He reign over you? Do you work for Him or merely for financial gain? Is He your God or is materialism?

These are just a few questions that all of your children could probably answer even if you have not discussed these issues with them. You don't have to. They know what matters to you simply by observing your example.

Examples to Remember in Hard Times

Timothy was encouraged to remember the teachings and example of his mother and grandmother when he was confronted with evil and falsehood (2 Tim. 3:13–15). The Hebrew Christians were reminded of the "cloud of witnesses" that surrounded them, whose faithful examples encourage others to persevere in the faith (Heb. 11:1–12:1). The same faltering Hebrew Christians were commanded to "remember those who led you, who spoke the word of God to you . . . imitate their faith" (Heb. 13:7). The steadfast examples of others give us strength in times of weakness throughout our entire lives.

During a recent visit by my parents-in-law to the home, I asked Dad and Mom to share their testimonies with us. I wanted my children to hear from their grandparents' lips how good God had been to them. One of Dad's stories has stuck in our minds, although Debby and I had not previously heard it and probably would never have learned of it had we not coerced her parents to talk about themselves that night.

Many years ago Dad completed some graduate studies at the University of Michigan in business administration. Afterwards, in the spring of 1948, when he and Mom lived in Southern California, there were tremendous prospects for development in the city of Glendale, and Dad decided to take advantage of an opening for public service. He sat down with several others to take the civil service exam so that he could be placed in the area of his greatest strength. As he took the test, a strange thing happened. He began to feel very uneasy about dedicating his life to building the city of Glendale. Though nearly finished with the test, he stood up under great conviction from God, put down his pencil, and walked out of the room! He was convinced that he should devote his life to building the kingdom of God rather than a city in Southern California. Dad had been considering pursuing the Christian ministry as his vocation. Now, suddenly, he was certain that he should do nothing else.

When he returned home, he told Mom what he had decided. Remarkably, she was totally supportive. To this day he cannot remember a single objection or complaint from her. And so, by that autumn, Dad and Mom were on the East Coast, where he enrolled in seminary.

It's hard to describe the impact that story has had on me and my family. Dad was in line for a successful career in the area for which he was trained. All the prospects looked great. But he and Mom were sensitive to the leading of the Holy Spirit and put Christ's church ahead of their own aspirations and dreams.

Today my children look with admiration on their grandparents as much as my wife and I do. Dad and Mom have given both us and our children a godly example to remember.

Who will remember *you* when he or she is tempted to waver? Whose faith will find strength in the example of your life? Will your children or grandchildren reflect on your godly example and be encouraged to persevere in faith, just as you have? Thank God that we don't have to be perfect to maintain His blessings on our homes. Because Jesus was perfect in our place, we can readily confess our sins to God—and to our children. God accepts and blesses our imperfect example for their benefit. As we lean on Jesus for grace, even the humble, inconsistent example of parents can serve as a bridge, rather than a stumbling block, to the gospel.

Discussion Questions

1. Can you think of a person whose example has dramatically affected you? What examples in the Bible have most impressed you? Why?
2. Discuss the power of your parents' example in your home as you grew up. Was it mainly positive? Why?
3. Discuss the importance of love for God in our being effective examples for our children.

❖ Chapter Nine ❖

The Prayers of Parents

Augustine of Hippo (A.D. 354–430) was one of the most instrumental leaders in the history of the Christian church. Through tireless preaching, teaching, and writing he defended and preserved for future generations the true doctrine of salvation by grace through faith alone. The Reformers of the sixteenth century praised his works as having had a significant impact on their rediscovering of biblical Christianity.

But this great Christian did not always lead a holy life. He was born of an unbelieving father and a believing mother. His mother could not restrain him from following the unbridled life of sin that his father's paganism encouraged. Augustine joined a cult, lived in sexual immorality, and fathered a son, traveling from city to city without lasting satisfaction. His mother, Monica, could hardly keep up with her wayward son. But her prayers followed him in earnest. Augustine's diary of his sinful youth (in his *Confessions*) depicts the fervent prayers of his believing mother. However bad things became, she could always be counted on to help him. She never gave up praying for his soul.

84

His conversion finally came in 386 in Milan, Italy, far away from his native northern Africa. Though he had been deeply influenced by the evangelical Bishop Ambrose of that city, Ambrose knew that the driving force in Augustine's conversion was more than *his* brief relationship with the young man. Upon hearing of Monica's strong faith and ceaseless prayers for her son, Ambrose said, "The son of so many prayers could not be lost." Monica persevered in faith and eventually received the promise of God in the salvation of her household, for even Patricius, her husband, was converted shortly before his death in 372.

Prayer is a parent's most potent weapon in raising a Christian family. Satan rejoices if he can get parents to think that their children will be saved through training and church attendance alone. But, as the rhyme says,

> The Devil trembles when he sees,
> The weakest saint upon his knees.

In this chapter we will focus on prayer in two ways: first, what prayer can accomplish, and second, the duty of prayer in the Christian home.

What Can Prayer Accomplish?

God uses prayer to change things. It is a gift to believers through which they have access to the power and blessings of God. The following texts express God's disposition toward His praying people. As you read them, resist the temptation to move on too quickly. Take a moment to let these verses sink in.

> The LORD is near to all who call upon Him, to all who call upon Him in truth. He will fulfill the desire of those who fear Him; He will also hear their cry and save them. (Ps. 145:18–19)

The sacrifice of the wicked is an abomination to the LORD, but the prayer of the upright is His delight. (Prov. 15:8)

The LORD longs to be gracious to you. . . . He will surely be gracious to you at the sound of your cry; when He hears it, He will answer you. (Isa. 30:18–19)

Call to Me, and I will answer you, and I will tell you great and mighty things, which you do not know. (Jer. 33:3)

Ask, and it shall be given to you; seek, and you shall find; knock, and it shall be opened to you. For everyone who asks receives, and he who seeks finds, and to him who knocks it shall be opened. (Matt. 7:7–8)

Again I say to you, that if two of you agree on earth about anything that they may ask, it shall be done for them by My Father who is in heaven. For where two or three are gathered together in My name, there I am in their midst. (Matt. 18:19–20)

All things you ask in prayer, believing, you shall receive. (Matt. 21:22)

Truly, truly, I say to you, if you shall ask the Father for anything, He will give it to you in My name. Until now you have asked for nothing in My name; ask, and you will receive, that your joy may be made full. (John 16:23–24)

Beloved, if our heart does not condemn us, we have confidence before God; and whatever we ask we receive from Him, because we keep His commandments and do the things that are pleasing in His sight. (1 John 3:21–22)

Are these promises true? Of course they are. They must be, or the Bible is a fraud. But God's Word cannot lie. A promise is a promise. And notice how wide in scope these promises are—they encompass everything. When problems arise in any area of life, we can pray about them and have confidence that God will hear us if we come to Him sincerely in Christ's name. Praying "in Christ's name" does not mean simply tagging those words onto the end of our prayers. It means actually praying for the praise of Christ and the advancement of His will, as well as praying with confidence that His mediation assures an answer from the Father. Jesus said, "And whatever you ask *in My name*, that will I do, *that the Father may be glorified in the Son*" (John 14:13).

When needs concerning our families arise, what, then, should we first do? Call the pastor? Call Dad or Mom for counsel? Turn to the index in the latest book on parenting to find out what the experts say? No. However useful these sources may be, we should first pray to God.

That truth was impressed on me recently in our morning family worship. I have a little devotional book that gives a Bible text, a poem, and a few thoughts on the text for each day. I read these few words and interact with Debby and the children about the text for a few minutes before we pray. The entry for that particular day included these words: "'David encouraged himself in the Lord his God.'—1 Sam. 30:6. When all within us is dark, and all around us is depressing, then is the time to turn from everything to God, and seek happiness only in him."

The strength we need ultimately comes from the Lord Himself, not man. We all fail each other daily, but our God can never fail. Whether he meets our needs directly or through other people, He is the one we can, and must, depend on. It only makes sense to go to Him *first* when facing any difficulty.

The promises of God concerning prayer are as relevant today as when He first spoke them. Notice that they do not say, "Whatever you ask for, *besides the salvation of your children*, you shall have." Included in all of these promises is the promise of salvation for those for whom we biblically intercede—including our children. Why do we pray for anyone's salvation unless we believe that our prayers are an important means God uses to save the one for whom we are praying? Why do we pray for anything unless we believe that it is a means ordained by God to achieve His ends through us?

Let's be honest. Most of us are horribly inconsistent concerning prayer. And one reason that we do not "pray without ceasing" is that we are not convinced that prayer works. We doubt the power of prayer because our prayers are not answered as quickly as we would like. It is as if we have defined effective prayer only in terms of quick results. But that is not God's idea of prayer. He does not promise always to answer immediately. He wants us to learn spiritual stamina to persist in long periods of prayer and not give up (Luke 18:1–8).

We forget that anything worth asking for once is worth asking for until we receive it. Our giving up suggests that our request is not a real need. James uncovered the root of the problem when he wrote: "You do not have because you do not ask. You ask and do not receive, because you ask with wrong motives, so that you may spend it on your pleasures" (James 4:2–3).

God's Sympathetic Ear

Too many of us have reached a point of doubting that God wants to meet our needs in answer to our prayers. What's the use, we ask? Such an attitude betrays a basic misunderstanding of the nature of God and hinders our relationship with Him. Earlier we noted that the author of Hebrews wrote, "Without faith it is impossible to please Him, for he who comes to God must believe that He is, *and that He is a rewarder of those who seek Him*" (Heb. 11:6).

Whenever we pray, we must believe that God is just who He has revealed Himself to be. He is the same eternal God today that He was in the days of Adam, Moses, Daniel, Paul, and John. This God is a fair and just God. He does not "lead us on." He is a rewarder of those who seek Him. He is sympathetic to our needs! We must believe this when we go to Him in prayer. We do not have to impress Him with fancy words or marathon prayers. He already is disposed to hearing and answering us. "For we do not have a high priest who cannot sympathize with our weaknesses. . . . Let us therefore draw near with confidence to the throne of grace, that we may receive mercy and find grace to help in time of need" (Heb. 4:15–16).

I remember praying that God would save my oldest brother's wife. Joyce was a wonderful southern girl whom Ralph had met while she was in college, but she was not a Christian. (My older brothers were set in their ways when my parents were converted, and so Ralph did not become genuinely interested in the Lord until after he had married.) Joyce and Ralph were visiting, and she had been impressed with the depth of my parents' faith.

I was in my early teens, and I simply believed that God would answer my prayer and save her. So I asked her if she wanted to receive Christ as her Lord and Savior. She responded that she did not know enough about the Bible. That didn't discourage me. I told her what she needed to know and to believe in order to become a child of God. And then I asked her again if she wanted to receive God's gift of eternal life. And she believed! Right then and there she prayed and was saved. So many Christians pray for the salvation of others but refuse to invite them to Christ when they have the opportunity. I was taught that God loved to answer prayer, even prayers for the salvation of others.

Praying with Faith

God tells us that He will answer our prayers offered in faith from a sincere heart for Christ's glory. But James states:

> If any of you lacks wisdom, let him ask of God, who gives to all men generously and without reproach, and it will be given to him. But let him ask in faith *without any doubting*, for the one who doubts is like the surf of

the sea driven and tossed by the wind. For let not that man expect to receive anything from the Lord. (James 1:5–7)

Where does strong faith come from? Is it a mystical feeling that sporadically seizes an individual and fills him with total assurance that God will grant exactly what he has prayed for? Is it a once-in-a-week experience? Did God intend for prayers of faith to be a rarity in our spiritual lives? No. Since God wants us to live by prayer continuously (see Luke 18:1; 1 Thess. 5:17), and true prayer requires faith, we can conclude that God wants us to be filled with faith at all times. We know that faith is the gift of God (Eph. 2:8). It cannot be worked up or produced by man. How then can we be filled with faith every time we pray? How can we know that God is pleased with our requests? God has answered that question.

Praying According to God's Will

John wrote: "This is the confidence which we have before Him, that, if we ask anything according to His will, He hears us. And if we know that He hears us in whatever we ask, we know that we have the requests which we have asked from Him" (1 John 5:14–15). This text teaches that everything we ask for in accordance with God's will shall be given. Perhaps you are thinking, *Thanks a lot. That doesn't help me at all, because who knows God's will, except God?* But don't miss the point John is making. He is saying that we can know God's will and pray for it. And that is exactly what gives us confidence "in whatever we ask" (v. 15).

What does John mean by "His will"? John uses that phrase one other time in this letter: "And the world is passing away, and also its lusts; but the one who does the will of God abides forever" (1 John 2:17). By "the will of God," John is referring not to God's secret and eternal will—which no one knows but God Himself—but to the revealed will of God, expressed in the Word of God. God's secret plan belongs to Him alone, but what He has revealed belongs to us forever (Deut. 29:29). We are to live by it. We are to pray by it. We can know what God's revealed will is.

Paul prayed that the Colossians would "be filled with the knowledge of His will in all spiritual wisdom and understanding" (Col. 1:9). That is precisely what John was saying. When we use God's Word as our source for the content of our prayers, we will always pray "according to His will." Jesus taught the same thing when He said, "If you abide in Me *and my words abide in you*, ask whatever you wish, and it shall be done for you" (John 15:7).

One very powerful way to pray, then, is to ask God to do for you what, according to His revelation, He desires to do for His children. When David prayed concerning his preparation for building the temple, he said, "Now therefore, O LORD God, the word that Thou hast spoken concerning Thy servant and his house, confirm it forever, *and do as Thou hast spoken*" (2 Sam. 7:25). That is the essence of praying according to God's will: "Do as You have said You will do, in such a way and at such a time as will bring You the most glory."

It is our wonderful and solemn privilege to use God's Word to "remind" Him of what He has promised. Isaiah 62:6–7 captures this concept: "On your walls, O Jerusalem, I have appointed watchmen; all day and all night they will never keep silent. You who remind the LORD, take no rest for yourselves; and give Him no rest until He establishes and makes Jerusalem a praise in the earth." Though our prayers should not be impatient demands, but humble requests, still we should pray until the answer comes. Those who persevere in such an intercessory ministry will not be disappointed, for it is the very Spirit of God who gives us the grace to persevere in prayer. He directs our minds to those portions of God's revealed will for which we are to pray.

Prayer as Spiritual Warfare

The Enemy of God is routed by the Christ-centered spiritual warfare of God's children. At the very heart of our warfare is praying with the Word of God. The Word is the "sword of the Spirit." Paul exhorts us to "take the helmet of salvation, and the sword of the Spirit, which is the word of God. With all prayer and petition pray at all times in the Spirit" (Eph. 6:17–18).

Take the Word and pray. God has given us His will in His Word. Claim every promise; plead every Word back to Him until He answers. Such prayers will always yield a fruitful harvest. And in this way "the God of peace will soon crush Satan under your feet" (Rom. 16:20).

Elijah is a good example of praying back to God what He has promised in His Word. Why would Elijah pray earnestly that it would not rain for three and a half years? A rather cruel prayer, wasn't it? Didn't Elijah know that untold suffering and death would result from his prayer? Why would he pray in this way? And why would God answer such a prayer? Elijah was motivated by his love for God. He said, "I have been very zealous for the LORD" (1 Kings 19:10). And the reason he prayed for drought was that God, through Moses, had threatened to bring drought if His children forsook Him:

> Beware, lest your hearts be deceived and you turn away and serve other gods and worship them. Or the anger of the LORD will be kindled against you, and He will shut up the heavens so that there will be no rain and the ground will not yield its fruit; and you will perish quickly from the good land which the LORD is giving you. (Deut. 11:16–17)

Israel forsook the Lord and worshiped Baal. Yet the rains continued to fall. The appearance was that the God of Israel could not back up His threats. Then "a man with a nature like ours" (James 5:17) began to pray. Elijah knew the promise and prayed it back to God. God waited to fulfill His Word until this man asked Him to do what He had promised. And how mightily He used Elijah to crush Satan's stronghold!

The Lord likewise waits on parents to claim the promises that He has made for their children. How pitiful it is to see

Satan dissolve Christian families in which parents do not oppose him in spiritual warfare. God's promises cannot fail. But you must believe and claim them.

Does Satan want your children? your spouse? You can be certain he does. Is there anything that you can do to thwart him from devouring them? Yes, there is, praise God! The Lord has revealed that it is His will for believers and their families to be saved. He has promised parents that He will be not only their God, but the God of their children, too. If you believe God's promise, then entreat God to do as He has said: save your family from their sins and put them on the path of righteousness and blessing. Such prayer is your most effective tool in bringing God's blessing on your entire household. (For more information on spiritual warfare, see my book *Miracles, Demons, and Spiritual Warfare: An Urgent Call for Discernment* [Grand Rapids: Baker, 1990]).

God Answers in His Timing

But remember, God has not promised to answer you immediately. As John Witherspoon, the only minister to sign the Declaration of Independence, observed:

> I could tell you some remarkable instances of parents who seemed to labor in vain for a long time, and yet were so happy as to see a change at last; and of some children in whom even after the death of the parents, the seed which was early sown, and seemed to have been entirely smothered, has at last produced fruit. (*The Works of John Witherspoon*, 3:499–500)

Persevere in praying for your family's conversion until you see it come to pass. Do not doubt for a moment that God will answer your prayer. It is His revealed will that your family be saved. He will bring it to pass in His time. He is sympathetic to your heart's desire for your family. In fact, He has placed that very desire inside you, and He is giving you the desire to pray for your family's salvation. "For it is God who is at work in you, both to will and to work for His good pleasure" (Phil. 2:13).

In this glorious way we see God's sovereign election working through the means of a parent's prayer. Our sovereign God ordains the means as well as the results. He knows who will be saved and how they will be saved. The specific details are all part of His remarkable plan. And every part of God's bringing salvation into our lives is solely of His grace.

We therefore must not be filled with pride when our prayers are answered, or with despair if they are not answered as quickly as we wish. We can persevere in prayer only by God's grace. And if we persevere in true believing prayer, we will forever glorify His name, not ourselves. Even when we are the instruments used of God to draw others to Christ, it is all of grace. Grace does away with both the vanity of pride and the vanity of despair. So, in your prayers, as well as in your walk, "Be steadfast, immovable . . . knowing that your toil is not in vain in the Lord" (1 Cor. 15:58).

Prayer in the Home

Family Harmony

In his inspired message to wives and husbands (1 Peter 3:1–7), Peter makes a startling comment about prayer in the home: "You husbands likewise, live with your wives in an understanding way, as with a weaker vessel, since she is a woman; and grant her honor as a fellow heir of the grace of life, *so that your prayers may not be hindered*" (v. 7). Prayer in the home is so important that Peter reminds us to guard against anything that might arise between a husband and wife and hinder their prayers.

Wrong attitudes, hurt feelings, misunderstandings, a lack of communication, unwillingness to forgive, and other such problems are all obstacles to united and persevering prayer in the home. The damage done by these stumbling blocks is incalculable. As much as they hurt the relationship between a husband and his wife, that is a small part of the consequences of such marital rifts. The worse damage is what happens to the united prayers of a husband and wife. God's promises are abandoned, and Satan is given a special opportunity to work his ruin in the home (Eph. 4:26–27).

Satan knows the effectiveness and power of prayer. He is fully aware of God's predisposition to answering the prayers of His children. So he does all he can to bring disharmony and alienation into Christian marriages. To the extent that he keeps partners from praying together, their homes are eternally affected.

Commenting on 1 Peter 3:7, Thomas Scott wrote:

[Husbands] should also more attentively guard against all disagreements and domestic uneasiness; that nothing might occur to indispose them from prayer, in secret, and in the family, *but especially with each other*. This, being essential to the Christian's prosperity, was a matter of so great importance, that all things, in his whole conduct, ought to be regulated with reference to it. . . .

Thus husbands and wives will be enabled to live together, "as fellow-heirs of the grace of life," and nothing will hinder their united prayers for a blessing upon each other, upon their children and family, and all who are connected with them. (*The Holy Bible with Explanatory Notes, Practical Observations and Copious Marginal References*, 3:860, 862, emphasis added)

How blind we are to the schemes of our "adversary, the devil, [who] prowls about like a roaring lion, seeking someone to devour" (1 Peter 5:8)! We allow disunity to affect our relationships with our spouses, thinking ignorantly that it will all resolve itself in time. Meanwhile our guard is down, and our homes are spiritually unprotected. We disregard family prayer, never imagining the ruin that will result among our children.

Where are the fathers today who dedicate themselves to praying for their families? Where are the partners who faithfully intercede for their children's spiritual and physical welfare day after day?

Persistence in Prayer

Jesus introduced the parable of the persistent widow "to show [the disciples] that they should always pray and not give up" (Luke 18:1, NIV). At the end of the parable, the Lord ominously stated, "However, when the Son of Man comes, will He find faith on the earth?" (v. 8). The context of these words suggests that the faith that will be practically nonexistent when Christ returns is the faith to cry out to God, the faith to pray without fainting.

Prayerlessness is a major problem of our day. Christians have time to do everything under the sun *except* pray. Yet we are commanded to "pray without ceasing" (1 Thess. 5:17; cf. Phil. 4:6). Why does God command us to constantly arm ourselves with prayers (Eph. 6:18)? Because we need them. And what we need as individuals we need even more as families.

It isn't enough to dedicate ourselves to biblical instruction, discipline, and being consistent examples in our homes if we omit prayer. Nor is it enough just to pray while forsaking our other responsibilities. A heart that has all four major arteries clogged needs quadruple bypass surgery. To clear up one artery will help for a while, but full and lasting health will not result unless all four arteries are working. The same is true of the health of our families. All four parental duties are vital to the health and strength of the family.

Prayer and Humility

Prayer best expresses an attitude of Christian humility. It is in prayer that parents admit their inability to change their child's heart, despite their best efforts. It is through prayer that parents confess their sins to God and find forgiveness through

Christ. And it is especially through the Word and prayer that the faltering faith of parents is strengthened and their resolve is quickened. In prayer we view the perfection of our Savior and remember, "It is finished!" (John 19:30).

There is no place for works-righteousness in the prayers of true Christians. All our best efforts apart from Him are nothing better than filthy rags (Isa. 64:6). But prayer keeps us from living apart from Him. Without prayer, parents could be deluded into thinking that *their* teaching, *their* discipline, *their* examples will all avail in the sure salvation of their children. But the praying parent realizes that salvation comes from above.

Charles Spurgeon said:

> How can a man be a Christian, and not love his offspring? How can a man be a believer in Jesus Christ, and yet have a cold and hard heart in the things of the kingdom, towards his children? . . . it is our business to train up our children in the fear of the Lord; and though we cannot give them grace, it is ours to pray to the God who can give it; and in answer to our many supplications, he will not turn us away, but will be pleased to regard our sighs. (*20 Centuries of Great Preaching,* 6:93–94)

How thankful we should be for the promises of God to our families! How grateful, also, that He has clearly spelled out our duties in this family covenant. We must look to Him for the grace needed to instruct, to discipline, to model, and to pray.

When Paul spoke of the *"grace in which we stand"* (Rom. 5:2), he pictured God and man at work together. Although we utterly depend on God's grace, nevertheless it is we who must stand. And His grace enables us to do that. So let us dedicate ourselves to performing all of our parental duties in a spirit of prayerful expectation, a hope rooted in the goodness of our Father and the righteousness of Christ.

Discussion Questions

1. How seriously have you taken the promises of God concerning prayer? How seriously should you take them? What changes should you make in your life in this regard?
2. Does God really care about your needs? Do you truly believe that He cares when you pray? Why doesn't He help you more often?
3. Where does faith come from?
4. What is "praying according to God's will"? Why don't Christians often pray according to God's will?
5. Can we believe in both the sovereignty of God and the power of prayer? If so, how?
6. How can you better mobilize yourself and others in spiritual warfare for your families?
7. Why is prayer so often neglected in Christian homes?
8. Why does God bless prayer?

❖ Chapter Ten ❖

Focus on Fathers

Not long ago a major greeting card producer teamed up with a local prison ministry to offer free Mother's Day cards to every inmate who wanted to send one to his mother. The response was astonishing, and the ministry had to do some last-minute ordering to meet the demand. Few had expected such a positive reaction.

Thrilled with this response, the ministry and the card supplier decided to make the same offer for Father's Day. They stockpiled a large quantity of cards, not wanting to be caught shorthanded again. They were even more flabbergasted this time around, but for a very different reason. Not a single inmate wanted to write home for Father's Day!

For some reason, fatherhood is not given the same regard as motherhood in our society. There is a general lack of appreciation of fatherhood even among fathers themselves. Men are abandoning their families at alarming rates. Of those who stay with their families, many abandon their responsibilities. Very few men welcome and seek to fulfill the biblical description of their role as fathers.

Where are Christian fathers today who lead their homes according to God's Word? It is tempting to say, "Well, I'm not as bad as the next guy." But we will all be judged by God's standard, not our neighbor's. How well do we fulfill the duties God has placed on believing fathers? How do we measure up to His Word? Paul made it clear that no other measure or comparison will do: "We are not bold to class or compare ourselves with some of those who commend themselves; but when they *measure themselves by themselves*, and *compare themselves with themselves*, they are without understanding" (2 Cor. 10:12).

Since we will stand before Jesus, what really matters is that we comply with His will. We who are fathers should so order our lives that when we appear before Him, we will be able to do so with joy instead of with sorrow. Will the blood of our children be on our hands? Or will the judgment reveal that our best efforts were devoted to their best interests?

Turning a Father's Heart to His Children

The Old Testament closes with the prediction of a coming day of revival. Malachi pictured that wonderful era in the following way: "And he will restore the hearts of the fathers to their children, and the hearts of the children to their fathers, lest I come and smite the land with a curse" (Mal. 4:6). Along with revival, this verse also alludes to God's judgment on a people and their land, during which their families are severed and the hearts of fathers and their children are worlds apart. All around us are homes divided in this way. Part of the reviving work of the Spirit of God is the healing of these homes. How does the Spirit accomplish such a healing according to this verse? The Holy Spirit uses the Word of God to turn the hearts of the fathers back to their children.

Fathers, has that happened to you? Where is your heart today? What is the desire and delight of your life? Is it your career? your home? your reputation? your finances? your sexual gratification? Or is it your family and the Lord?

Countless children wake up filled with sorrow or anger because their fathers have abandoned them. That abandonment takes many forms. We may live under the same roof and bring home a paycheck, but if we do not delight in and live for our children, we have *functionally* abandoned them. They long for a father's attention and love. As Solomon said, "The glory of sons is their fathers" (Prov. 17:6). When a child loses that delight in his father, the breach is serious. How can it be restored? Malachi said that when the fathers' hearts are turned back to their children, then the children's hearts will turn back to their fathers.

The wonderful movie *Field of Dreams* begins with Ray Kinsella talking about his father. Ray's alienation from his father is the underlying theme of the film. At fourteen, Ray refused to play catch with his dad, who had pushed him too hard to excel at baseball. And at seventeen, Ray ran away and did not see his father again. He laments that he was too stubborn to humble himself and try to bridge the gulf between them. Not until the end of the film does Ray realize that the words "If you build it, he will come" and "Ease his pain" refer to the return of his father, and not "Shoeless" Joe Jackson's coming to play ball on Ray's "dream" field.

The film peaks when Ray's father returns as a young ballplayer. The two talk briefly, but Ray does not fully identify himself. Then, as his father begins to walk away, Ray calls out to him, "Hey, Dad, you wanna play catch?" To this his father stops and replies with a knowing smile, "I'd like that!" These are the last words of this powerful movie. The camera slowly zooms out as father and son play catch, the father's heart turned to his son, and the son, with unrestrained delight, enjoying a much-longed-for moment of nearness to his dad.

It is an inexplicably powerful moment when a father turns his heart to his children—for the first time, or after he has drifted away. In this chapter we will consider how God intends fathers' hearts to be turned toward their children in terms of the four basic responsibilities of fathers: instructing, disciplin-

ing, modeling, and praying. I will offer some practical suggestions concerning how our torn homes can be mended.

Unless we fathers turn our hearts to our children in ways
commanded by God, we will likely lose our children to this
world, and we will certainly bring God's chastening upon ourselves. We constantly need His Spirit's work within us to make
our hearts soft, approachable, and teachable.

A Father's Instruction

Fathers bear the ultimate responsibility to teach their children
God's Word in the home. They are commanded to "bring them
up in the . . . instruction of the Lord" (Eph. 6:4). As I understand it, that implies several things.

1. *A Christian father should lead in the biblical instruction of his
family.* Husbands are prone to delegate their teaching duty
almost exclusively to their wives. That tendency seems to portray Christianity as an unmanly thing to their children. When
the children are young, mothers will likely have more opportunities to give them biblical training. But on the whole, fathers
should take the lead in the home in teaching and explaining
God's Word.

Where do fathers find the time needed to learn and to
train their children? That's a good question. David was a busy
king and warrior, and yet he found time to spend with his
children. He said, "Come, you children, listen to me; I will
teach you the fear of the Lord" (Ps. 34:11). And when his
son Solomon was older, he remembered David's instruction
and wrote:

> When I was a son to my father, tender and the only
> son in the sight of my mother, then he taught me and
> said to me, "Let your heart hold fast my words; keep
> my commandments and live; acquire wisdom! Acquire
> understanding! Do not forget, nor turn away from the

words of my mouth. Do not forsake her, and she will guard you; love her, and she will watch over you." (Prov. 4:3–6)

Though David was as busy as a father could be, he took time to instruct his son. We, too, must make time to teach our children.

Some of my best moments of teaching occur around the table and in the car. We almost always review the Sunday message on the way home from church. My children carefully write down the title and main points of the outline, knowing that I will quiz them. On a recent Sunday our nine-year-old surprised a visiting speaker by showing him her notes on his sermon accompanied by her artistic illustrations.

Sometimes I just ask the kids to look around them and tell me what they are thankful for. Most of us have a lot more time for teaching than we realize. We just need to be better stewards of those many natural opportunities. Children grow up quickly, so take the time to train them while there is time.

2. *The training a father gives should be both formal and informal.* Dads should lead in formal times of daily family worship, often called "family devotions." That is a good time to study a few verses of God's Word and have plenty of discussion. Discussion keeps study from becoming boring, especially to children. Ask the Lord to help you develop the skill of asking questions that are relevant to your kids. Think of what is going on in each child's life and direct the discussion to that area. Try to be creative in your teaching, so that it never becomes drudgery. That will make all the difference in the world for your children's appreciation of family devotions.

Most of the training we provide as fathers will be informal. God should be part of all our discussions. Every aspect of life is to honor Him. Paul commanded, "Whether, then, you eat or drink or whatever you do, do all to the glory of God" (1 Cor. 10:31). Jesus made object lessons out of ordinary situations all around Him. So should we. If the psalmist teaches that "the heavens are telling of the glory of God" (Ps. 19:1), we too ought to learn to glorify God through His creation. You can show your children how grass grows better in the open sunlight than in the shade. Then apply this lesson to their lives by showing them how important God's Light (Jesus) is for spiritual health and how dangerous it is when anything obscures that Light from shining on them.

Children need to develop a sense of the closeness of God. Show them how all the things He brings into our lives glorify Him, "for from Him and through Him and to Him are all things. To Him be the glory forever. Amen" (Rom. 11:36). As fathers bring all their needs before God, they show their children how faithful God is to meet those needs. King Hezekiah serves as an example to us fathers: "It is the living who give thanks to Thee, as I do today; a father tells his sons about Thy faithfulness" (Isa. 38:19).

Some of the best times of spiritual growth we've had as a family have been periods of great trial. If our children were old enough to understand, we shared our trials with them, and we all sought God's help together. He has never failed us. Several times He has wonderfully blessed us for standing for His truth and has brought us out of trial and into great prosperity. As we have shared such experiences with our children, they have learned the faithfulness and love of *their* God.

In order to become God-centered adults, our children must know that God is interested in every aspect of their lives. If they lose something, we must teach them to pray that God will help them find it. If they are ill, we should pray with them for God's healing. Instruction alone cannot fully persuade them that everything related to their lives is important to their God. Our responses to life's challenges must reflect a constant Christ-centeredness. He must be a living and active Savior in our homes.

3. *Fathers have been commissioned to make disciples of their children (Matt. 28:19–20).* Jesus taught that one of the evidences of true discipleship is the desire to live a Bible-centered life: "If

you abide in My word, then you are truly disciples of Mine; and
you shall know the truth, and the truth shall make you free"
(John 8:31–32).

Fathers should teach the Word in such a way that their
children will want to "abide in it," or live by it. For this attitude
to take hold, kids need to understand the lordship of Christ
over their lives. If Jesus is their King, then they belong to His
kingdom, and the law that governs Christ's kingdom is the
Word of God. The Bible is far more than an interesting book
of meditations or inspiring stories. It is the Law of our King—
to be followed and obeyed. That leads to our next point.

4. *Fathers have a responsibility to make their children understand
that obeying Christ is nonnegotiable.* We *must* obey our King! It is
foolish and unsafe to do otherwise. Today's brand of Christianity lacks a sense of the necessity expressed so often in the New
Testament by the simple word *must*. We *must* be born again
(John 3:7). We *must* worship God in spirit and truth (John 4:24).
We *must* endure many tribulations before we enter heaven (Acts
14:22). We *must* help the weak (Acts 20:35). We *must* pay much
closer attention to the words of Jesus than the Israelites paid to
God's law (Heb. 2:1).

Our children need to be taught the imperative nature of
Christianity. Abraham was commended by God because he
would *"command* his children . . . to keep the way of the LORD
by doing righteousness and justice" (Gen. 18:19). Moses finished his solemn message to Israel by saying, "Take to your
heart all the words with which I am warning you today, *which
you shall command your sons to observe carefully,* even all the words
of this law. For it is not an idle word for you; indeed it is your
life" (Deut. 32:46–47).

The word for "command" used of Abraham and by
Moses in these passages is the word for charging or ordering
someone to do something. The same word is used by the
Lord when He says to Moses and again to Jeremiah, "You
shall speak all that I *command* you . . ." (Ex. 7:2; Jer. 1:7). A
command is not optional; it is obligatory. Failure to obey a

command causes serious consequences, simply because it *ought* to be obeyed.

Fathers need to command their children today, too. They should exercise their authority in a spirit of love, but the need for love does not lessen their children's obligation to follow the Lord's commands. In other words, fathers will need to show a degree of inflexibility. The children might wonder, "Do we have to pray before every meal?" Yes, we are taught to do so in God's Word (1 Tim. 4:3–5). They might wonder, "Must we have daily devotions?" Yes, the psalmist said, "In the morning, O LORD, Thou wilt hear my voice; in the morning I will order my prayer unto Thee and eagerly watch" (Ps. 5:3). And Jesus commanded us to pray that God would supply our *daily* bread. We need His grace every day.

One rule in our home is that the children do their homework when they first get home from school. When that is done, they can play. We do show flexibility when appropriate, but we have a general law, which serves a good, biblical purpose. The kids also know that I will spend a certain amount for their athletic shoes. I have explained to them Christ's teaching on financial responsibility and set a limit. If they want to get a more expensive pair, they pay the difference from their earnings. We always shop around and get a good deal. They have become more patient shoppers, especially when they are paying part of the price! Recently the Lord enabled us to find an outlet that sells most brands at half price. Now they rarely pay anything out of their own pockets. Someone must have been praying!

Our supreme law for life is the Word of Christ. He asked, "And why do you call Me, 'Lord, Lord,' and do not do what I say?" (Luke 6:46). Is He the Lord of your home? Do you teach and enforce His rules? Do you base your family regulations on the principles of Scripture? Do you explain that the reason you do not watch certain things on television is that they are forbidden by our King in His Word? Do you forbid your children to demean each other because Christ has told us that such talk is sin?

Fathers, explain to your children that some day you will

have to stand before God to give account of how you raised them. Their hearts respond to this, particularly if you do this at a time when you are not reprimanding them. They do not want Jesus to be disappointed with you. Let them see that Christ rules your home and that you, as well as they, are under His authority.

When they ask you why they cannot do something, be ready to show them from God's Word that He has said that it is wrong. You didn't make up the rules. They are God's rules, and you are seeking to apply them as best you can. Your children will grow to trust your judgment and submit to your authority. In their minds you have earned the right to their trust. You have drawn the boundaries clearly and shown that you are enforcing not your own whims but Jesus' rules. You have started commanding your children in a way that they will respond to, because it is apparent that Jesus is the Lawgiver. As fathers lovingly command their children to follow Jesus, while following Him themselves, they can expect more harmony and less rebellion in their homes. Let me illustrate.

My oldest daughter will be a junior in high school next year. We have discussed sexual issues together, and she and I have covenanted that she will never get romantically involved with a boy apart from my knowledge and approval. She wears a ring that symbolizes our agreement. One of my responsibilities is to meet with the boy and tell him my expectations, which includes discussing the subject of intimate physical contact. We believe that Paul teaches that intimate physical contact should not occur outside marriage (1 Cor. 7:1). For us, then, the American way of dating is unacceptable because it allows for some intimate physical contact, which very often leads to sexual intercourse.

My beautiful daughter knows that I want only the best for her. She understands that our agreement is rooted in our attempt to apply the Bible to our lives today. Instead of driving her away from me, our agreement has deepened her trust in me. She sees again that I truly want to lead our family by the law of our King. I don't know that my covenant with her is for everyone. In fact, I'm not certain what form of agreement I will make with my other children when they are older. They are all unique. I am sure, though, that as I seek God's wisdom, He will lead me. And they respect my desire to follow Him with their good in mind.

5. *Fathers should lead their families in memorizing God's Word.* At the beginning of the week Dad can assign a weekly Bible verse for the family—and everyone can learn it together. Memorization is important. The Spirit of God often uses memorized Bible verses to keep us from evil and to deliver us from temptation. David said, "Thy word I have treasured [hidden] in my heart, that I may not sin against Thee" (Ps. 119:11).

Often while I am watching sports on television, a sexually suggestive commercial comes on. Two verses often come to my mind: "Do not let your heart turn aside to her ways, do not stray into her paths. For many are the victims she has cast down, and numerous are all her slain" (Prov. 7:25–26). It is interesting that these words of warning were spoken by a father to his sons (v. 24; see also Job 31:1; Matt. 5:28). When a suggestive commercial is played on TV, my son and I simply turn our attention away until it is over.

Resisting temptation is just one of the many good reasons to memorize Scripture. Our kids also need to be reminded of biblical principles that will help them make good decisions, such as the many other principles stated in memorable form in the Proverbs. Memorizing Scripture also equips children to spot and refute wrong ideas. And perhaps most importantly, it reminds them of who they are, why they are here, and how much they must depend on the Lord for forgiveness, strength, and life itself.

6. *In order to teach their children well, fathers need to be constantly learning.* If you do not deepen your own understanding, your well of truth will dry up. Use every possible means to grow in grace and in the knowledge of God. Read the Bible daily. Buy good Christian books. Listen to Christian radio broadcasts that faithfully teach the Word and help you apply its timeless truths

to your personal life. There are some broadcasts that specialize on the family that you may find very helpful. And, of course, don't neglect the teaching and preaching of the Word available at your church. Try taking notes on the Sunday sermons and carefully applying them to your life. Your own well needs to be replenished in order for you to draw from it fresh teaching for your family. Seek every opportunity to refill your supply of life-giving truth.

May the Lord help us fathers dedicate ourselves to our great duty of teaching. It is for our own benefit as well as that of our families. What Paul urged Timothy applies as well to us: "Pay close attention to yourself and to your teaching; persevere in these things; for as you do this you will insure salvation both for yourself and for those who hear you" (1 Tim. 4:16).

A Father's Discipline

The Lord has commanded fathers to discipline their children in a particular way: "Fathers, do not provoke your children to anger; but bring them up in the discipline and instruction of the Lord" (Eph. 6:4). In this verse Paul qualifies a Christian father's discipline in three respects:

1. *A father's discipline must not provoke anger in his children.* In the parallel text, Colossians 3:21, Paul states, "Fathers, do not exasperate your children, that they may not lose heart." One common way fathers exasperate their children is by over-disciplining. The punishment must suit the crime. It is unjust to punish a child before doing a thorough investigation to see whether a willful offense has been committed. We fathers tend to react to situations and therefore hastily discipline our kids without proper investigation. That is *not* the discipline of the Lord.

God is infinitely just, never punishing or chastening out of proportion to the offense. If we are to be fair to our children, we need to listen to their explanations before we draw conclusions. Often I have wrongly disciplined my children in haste, only to discover later that the "offense" was not a deliberate act of sin. I have had to go to them and confess my misjudgment, asking for their and My heavenly Father's forgiveness.

There is a significant difference between a deliberate act of sin and a childish accident. They should *not* be punished in the same way. Sins often cause the consciences of children to be struck with guilt. Feeling this, kids sense that a price has to be paid for their sins. When they are fairly punished by a prayerful, self-controlled parent, a deep sense of forgiveness and healing results. The child may actually feel better as a result. But the child who is severely punished for an accident or misunderstanding feels a strong sense of injustice. This exasperates the child and can result in deep bitterness and resentment against the parent. Though getting the facts is much easier said than done, fathers must be especially mindful of the danger of jumping to conclusions at the expense of fairness and a healthy relationship with their children.

2. *Ephesians 6:4 also says that fathers should "bring them up" in godly discipline.* The phrase "bring them up" implies a constant influence, rather than a temporary or sporadic one. Discipline should be a regular, continuous feature of the Christian home. Consistency is the key. Children should learn that God's rules do not change because He and His Word do not change. When they transgress the divine standard, there must be discipline. They need to expect that their sins will surely find them out (Num. 32:23). Their learning early in life that sin has consequences will lay a foundation for a better understanding and appreciation of what Jesus' death has done for sinners. They will likely understand *why* He had to die. If their sins are not consistently dealt with by firm and loving discipline, your children may not understand why Jesus' payment for sin is so precious and important.

3. *Paul also tells us that a father's discipline should be "the discipline of the Lord."* A father's discipline ought to imitate our

heavenly Father's discipline of His children. God's discipline concerns more than justice. It is primarily an expression of His love for His children: "Those whom the Lord loves He disciplines, and He scourges every son whom He receives" (Heb. 12:6).

God does not ignore our sin until He can take no more and then blow His stack, crushing us with His clenched fist. God disciplines His children in love—always. How we fathers need to pray for grace to do the same! Children find their fathers' angry outbursts confusing. Recently, while I was correcting my son, he asked me, "Why are you so angry?" It was a good question. I am glad that my relationship with John is such that he could ask it. Many sons would be afraid to raise such a question at that moment. The truth is that I was sinning by reproving him without proper self-control.

Such moments of fatherly sin contradict the biblical notion of fatherhood. Though we might associate explosions of anger with manhood, they are really the eruptions of weak and depraved hearts. Many of us fathers have not confessed and forsaken the sin of uncontrolled, oppressive anger. When this ugly revelation exposes the dark side of our nature, there is only one thing to do. Deal with it. Seeking the wonderful, renewing power of the Holy Spirit's sanctification. Deal with it before you drive your children away from you—and from God.

Love also overlooks what can be overlooked. "A man's discretion makes him slow to anger, and it is his glory to overlook a transgression" (Prov. 10:12). Fathers can sometimes hound their children, especially teenagers, into frustration. Teenagers are undergoing tremendous physical and emotional changes, which sometimes make small things appear very big to them. Parents need to be sympathetic during this time of change, helping them through it instead of adding unnecessary stress. Peter wrote that "love covers a multitude of sins" (1 Peter 4:8). The wise father will be able to discern what issues need to be addressed and what can be overlooked without severe consequences. The key is to distinguish between your teen's deliberate disobedience and his or her personal preferences. We must let growing children develop their own uniqueness, however different from us that might be, provided their choices do not involve sin.

One of the worst things a father can do is leave all the discipline to his wife. Worst still is neglecting it altogether. Hebrews 12:9 says, "We have earthly fathers *to discipline us,* and we respect them." Do not forsake your duty, fathers, or think that your children will respect you more for tolerating their sins and rebellion. They will respect you for consistently disciplining them in love. They were designed by God to need discipline and to respect those who rightly administer it. They know that they are sinners and that sin deserves punishment. Children's entire perception of reality becomes distorted, therefore, when their fathers are permissive regarding their children's sin. What your kids need is a caring father, not just another pal who thinks everything they do is cool.

A Father's Example

Few examples are sadder than the following one:

> Amon was twenty-two years old when he became king, and he reigned two years in Jerusalem. . . . And he did evil in the sight of the LORD, *as Manasseh his father had done.* For *he walked in all the way that his father had walked, and served the idols that his father had served* and worshiped them. So he forsook the LORD, the God of his fathers, and did not walk in the way of the LORD. (2 Kings 21:19–22)

We cannot overestimate the power of a father's example in the home. Just as children bear the genetic likeness of their parents, so they usually are a striking image of the moral character of their parents. How careful, then, a father should be in all aspects of his life!

Our words and deeds are performed on the stage of our

homes, with our children as understudies. Day after day they view the performance. Will they be unaffected by it? They can hardly not be. Should a father be surprised, then, if his children act the same way he has? Wasn't his the leading role in this daily performance?

A father's attitudes toward God, worship, money, character, women, work, and every other aspect of life are like a script that his children learn by heart over the years. And when, in adulthood, their time comes to take the lead, they will tend to reenact from memory what they observed in their fathers' lives. What power for evil or good an ordinary father possesses!

The psalmist said:

> I will walk within my house in the integrity of my heart. I will set no worthless thing before my eyes. . . . A perverse heart shall depart from me; I will know no evil. . . . My eyes shall be upon the faithful of the land, that they may dwell with me. . . . He who practices deceit shall not dwell within my house. (Ps. 101:2–4, 6–7)

In order to make our homes havens of holiness where our children will follow the way of the Lord, we fathers need to develop a fierce determination to walk in integrity and not practice deceit. We will need to be as resolute as Joshua was when he cried out:

> Now, therefore, fear the LORD and serve Him in sincerity and truth; and put away the gods which your fathers served beyond the River and in Egypt, and serve the LORD. And if it is disagreeable in your sight to serve the LORD, choose for yourselves today whom you will serve . . . but *as for me and my house, we will serve the LORD.* (Josh. 24:14–15)

Lead your homes as worthy examples. Make every effort to *show* as well as to teach what it means to serve the Lord.

A Father's Prayer

We have said a lot about prayer in the previous chapter. Fathers, do you believe that the following truths apply to your children?

- Nothing is impossible with prayer.
- Prayer is the spiritual pipeline through which the blessings of God flow to His people.
- Prayer is our greatest weapon against sin and Satan.
- We should always pray and never give up (Luke 18:1).
- We are commanded to pray without ceasing (1 Thess. 5:17).
- Prayer is the means by which believers claim all the promises of God.
- Prayer is the best evidence of a Christian's spiritual health.

As a measure of your commitment to these truths, does a spirit of prayer permeate your home? If it does not, that indicates that you are spiritually weak and your home is extremely vulnerable. Let me explain.

Many of us *don't* pray more because we *can't* pray more. We aren't spiritually strong enough for the exercise of prayer. My thirteen-year-old son does seventy push-ups each night. I can't do that because my muscles can't sustain that amount of physical exercise. He didn't become that fit all at once. He had to work up to it gradually. Just as physical muscles need exercise to build up to a certain challenge, so our faith needs the spiritual exercise of prayer to become and stay well conditioned.

If we want our children to be healthy in their spiritual lives, they must be taught to pray. And they will not likely work at it more than their fathers do. In any form of exercise, we must be convinced of the benefits before we are willing to put in the effort. Few people do push-ups or sit-ups for the fun of it. So, our children must learn the benefits of spiritual exercise from us. That doesn't mean you should immediately try to pray all night—you'd likely suffer spiritual exhaustion. Begin instead with a few minutes, and increase your prayer as your desire increases. That will ensure that your prayers are motivated by your growing love for Jesus.

Our home has been wonderfully blessed as we have used the Lord's Prayer as our model in family worship each day. I have taught my four children the meaning of each request in the Lord's Prayer by praying with them. I amplify each petition enough to show them its relevance to their lives. Now they can pray that wonderful prayer with meaning and fullness. Jesus Himself taught His disciples to pray by using the same outline. If you follow His example, I guarantee that your home will be mightily changed, as ours has been, by praying as He has commanded us to each day.

Since all fathers are sinners, all fathers will fail in the areas of instruction, discipline, being examples, and prayer. But, as the hymn states, *Jesus never fails!* And that reality is the basis for our acceptance with God the Father. We, therefore, need not hesitate to confess our sinful failures. We can trust that Christ can and will transform us in these four key areas. Seek His strength to make the outward changes you must make, and trust Jesus to make the inward changes that He alone can produce. In the daily struggles of our homes, as in every other area of life, we can say with Paul, "I can do all things through Him who strengthens me" (Phil. 4:13).

Discussion Questions

1. Why is it unwise to compare our lives with the lives of those around us?
2. What is involved in fathers' turning their hearts toward their children? What are the source and the result of this turning?
3. Which of the six pointers concerning a father's instruction most impressed you? Why?

4. What are the three rules for discipline taught in Ephesians 6:4?

5. Discuss the elements of the Lord's discipline of His children and how these principles should be followed in your discipline.

6. Can you think of some fathers who greatly influenced their children by their examples for evil or good?

7. Which of the listed truths on prayer meant the most to you? Why?

8. Describe how you can become stronger in the exercise of prayer.

9. Why is it important to use the Lord's Prayer in family worship?

❖ CHAPTER ELEVEN ❖

A Word to Mothers

Lexie was the mother of a Texas football star who saw her son going farther and farther away from Christ as he moved up the ladder of success. A college All-American and early-round draft pick of the San Francisco 49ers, Bruce Collie was finally ready for the "big time." When this huge offensive lineman left for California, his mother slipped a copy of the Psalms into his suitcase and followed her son with her constant prayers.

Over a period of five years Bruce flourished with one of the most successful franchises in the National Football League. He owned the homes, the cars, the boat (and later even an airplane) that often accompany great wealth. The big bucks and celebrity status brought him all the attention and worldly opportunities that one could imagine. He even achieved the goal of winning two Super Bowl rings. With all the success, glamour, and hype of being an NFL champion, Bruce's life was one party after another. In the minds of many, he had "arrived." Yet he felt empty. The big time ended up being pretty small after all.

It was then that his mother's prayers were dramatically answered. Bruce started to lose his drive to play pro football.

He called Lexie in 1990 and said that he was coming home. When she asked him, "Well, Bruce, what are you going to do?" he began to cry. He didn't know what to do. She told him to start reading the copy of the Psalms she had given him and to wait on God. When Bruce read the first Psalm, he saw the picture of his life. He was walking in the counsel of the ungodly. He was like the wind-driven chaff. With tears, he gave his heart completely to Christ. He began to devour the Psalms. Then a surprising thing happened. He was cut by the team. Even more surprising was the fact that he really wasn't upset. He began to trust in the Lord to direct his life.

Within a few hours, Bruce was claimed by the Philadelphia Eagles, and he finished that season with them. When he wasn't practicing or eating, he was usually in his hotel room devouring the Word of God. The next year he married another new Christian, Holly, and they grew quickly in their faith together. Bruce's mom was ecstatic at the way God had delivered her son and given him a wonderful Christian mate.

In the summer of 1991, Bruce was interviewed by a local sportscaster and gave a clear testimony of his faith in the Lord. I heard the interview and was deeply impressed with this professional athlete who was associating himself so boldly with Jesus. So I wrote to him and encouraged him to continue following the Lord. One thing led to another, and quite unexpectedly I ended up discipling Bruce in the faith.

I have had the privilege of meeting Bruce's mom and dad. Lexie just beams as she hears her son share his faith. Following his retirement, Bruce and his wife Holly moved back to Texas and started a Christian sports camp. They have also started a wonderful Christian family with two daughters and a son. God rescued Bruce's life through the faithful prayers of his mother.

The average mother would have been so caught up in her son's physical success that she would not have even thought of his spiritual need. Instead of slipping a copy of the Psalms into his suitcase, she would have been calculating how she was going to help him spend all his newly acquired wealth! One big reason why Bruce Collie is serving the Lord is that his mother did not get caught up in his apparent success. She knew that her son's life would be miserable until Christ ruled it. Lexie Collie prayed, and God answered in ways far greater than she could ever have imagined.

I am of the opinion that most of the problems in Christian homes are due to fathers. If they would sincerely attempt to lead their families as they should, depending on God's grace, most of the difficulties in their homes would be resolved.

That, however, is not meant to diminish the significance of a mother's influence in the home or the importance of addressing evident weaknesses in the lives of Christian mothers. Many of the principles we have seen thus far apply as much to mothers as to fathers. Since I am not a mother, I will not pretend to be competent in the specifics of a mother's responsibilities regarding instruction, discipline, setting an example, and prayer. But I want to make a few biblically based remarks to the moms reading this book.

Your Children Need You

Lamenting Israel's captivity, Jeremiah cried, "Even jackals offer the breast, they nurse their young; but the daughter of my people has become cruel like ostriches in the wilderness" (Lam. 4:3). Comparing mothers with ostriches produces a disturbing analogy. The ancient Near Eastern impression of the ostrich was not very favorable, as Job suggests:

> The ostriches' wings flap joyously with the pinion and plumage of love, for she abandons her eggs to the earth, and warms them in the dust, and she forgets that a foot may crush them, or that a wild beast may trample them. She treats her young cruelly, as if they were not hers; though her labor be in vain, she is unconcerned; because God has made her forget wisdom, and has not given her a share of understanding. (Job 39:13–17)

Thus the ostrich, in biblical culture, represented irresponsibility and selfishness. It was quite unflattering for Jeremiah to liken the mothers of captive Israel to ostriches. And yet the analogy fit the Israelite mothers. They were guilty of gross selfishness, some having destroyed and even eaten their own children (Lam. 4:10)! Instead of nurturing and loving their children, they had turned against them to preserve their own existence.

The story has twentieth-century applications. Aren't some mothers today abandoning their children in favor of selfish pursuits? There are different ways for a mother to abandon her children. She can abandon them *literally*, as do the thousands of young mothers who are hooked on crack cocaine. Our family courts are flooded with cases in which grandmothers end up taking custody of children whose mothers won't care for them. We need to love, help, and pray for such mothers. And we should do all we can to rescue and nurture their children. Doesn't Christ love those children, too? But few Christians are merciful enough to step forward and start meeting this need. What will happen to the next generation when there are few godly grandmothers left to step in and rescue the children?

Thousands more mothers live under the same roofs as their children but, like the ostrich, *functionally* abandon them. For all practical purposes, their children are unsupervised and unguided. Life has gotten so busy and complex that there is little time left for nurturing, loving, caressing, listening to, and teaching these little ones.

No Place Like Home?

It would be unfair to implicate all mothers who work outside the home. Sometimes that is a necessity, and some mothers take great pains to see that their children are under good Christian day care or in another suitable arrangement. This is where the local church should step up and help care for those who need a hand. The elderly, singles, and more affluent families should become mobilized in a mercy ministry to working mothers in each congregation. There are many mothers who would love to stay at home with their children but cannot. These sisters need our understanding and love, not our blame.

But sometimes outside work is unnecessary. More moms could stay at home if Christian parents were not consumed by the American dream. Materialistic gain is the god of our age. This form of idolatry can be very tempting, but is it worth it to gain the world and lose your own children in the process?

Remember what Solomon said: "The rod and reproof give wisdom, but a child *left to himself* brings shame to his mother" (Prov. 29:15, NKJV). The mother who chooses to pursue her career at the expense of her children is setting an example that will likely be repeated in her daughters. And where will that trend take us in a generation or two?

Today, while we recognize the needs of some to work outside the home, we should highlight the honor of women who are career homemakers. The media and secular educators of our society have practically declared war on traditional motherhood. Many moms feel guilty or unfulfilled for staying home and taking care of the kids. Have American Christians adopted the standards of a materialistic culture instead of maintaining the words of their King? Undoubtedly many have, and we are paying dearly for it. We spend a fortune buying fancy things for our children and are surprised when they spend more time playing with the box than with the gift inside! What our kids need is *us*. They need *our attention* rather than the mere things we buy them to consume their time. We who are husbands need to express our love and appreciation for the unending work that our wives do in the home, instead of making them feel guilty for not getting an outside job.

Paul told older Christian women to teach "the young women to love their husbands, to love their children, to be sensible, pure, workers at home, kind, being subject to their own husbands, that the word of God may not be dishonored" (Titus 2:4–5). Despite current social pressures, we should not relegate this text to biblical times. If we lay the Word aside, we show dishonor to the One who gave it. When Eli did not heed God's Word in his home, God punished him, saying, "Those who honor Me I will honor, and those who despise Me will be lightly esteemed" (1 Sam. 2:30).

A big part of our problem is our expectations. We want too much too quickly for ourselves and our family. Our family budgets should be in line with the biblical standard of need and comfort instead of the American standard of excess and luxury (see Matt. 6:25–34; 2 Cor. 4:18; Phil. 4:11–13; 1 Tim. 6:6–10, 17–19). We buy far too much and then have to work extra to pay for it. Missiologist Jonathan Bonk explains:

> Anthropologist Jules Henry recognized the preoccupation with consumption . . . when he suggested that life in North America could be summed up by two great commandments: "Create more desire" and "Thou shalt consume." American well being, he argued, rested in the faithful obedience of the majority to these two imperatives.
>
> On the one hand, he pointed out, nothing could be more economically catastrophic than a decline in consumer demand. . . . Accordingly, consumers are "daily confronted with a barrage of advertising calculated to frighten or flatter them out of reasonable contentment into the nagging itch for goods and services [they] don't really need."
>
> On the other hand, new consumer cravings had to be discovered and created. Nothing could be more economically destructive than an outbreak of contentment. For the majority of North Americans to remain content with last year's shoes, hats, clothes, cars, furniture, electronic gadgets, breakfast cereals, detergents, perfumes, hair styles, and houses would spell the end of the "good life." (*Missions and Money,* 28)

The decision of a mother to leave the home is one of momentous consequences. How sad it is when that is done with little thought or no true necessity.

Often that decision reflects the level of a mom's (or a couple's) faith. Is God big enough to provide for those who resist self-advancement and who determine to live biblically? He certainly is, and He loves to show Himself strong and faithful to His Word. He owns the cattle on a thousand hills, and He is able to send one into your pasture when you need it. "For the eyes of the LORD move to and fro throughout the earth that He may strongly support those whose heart is completely His" (2 Chron. 16:9). So instead of determining your needs by looking at the possessions of your neighbors, let God's Word define your needs, and ask God to supply them. But do not forsake your duty towards your precious children.

To you dear sisters who would rather be at home with your children but feel you have no alternative than to work outside the home, let me offer some advice.

First, pray that God would have mercy on you and free you to spend more time with your children. Remember that He loves you and your children. You do not have to convince Him of your need. But He does want you to cry out for His assistance.

Second, go to your pastor, elder, deacon, or close Christian friend and share your burden with him or her. Be like the widow of Luke 18:1–7. Refuse to give up. If you persist, something will happen that will not only assist you but also help many other sisters like you. I pray with you that new mercy ministries to single mothers, out-of-home working mothers, and impoverished mothers will begin as a result of your courage and faith. Don't merely complain and think that your situation is hopeless. Nothing is impossible with God! Act today for your children's sake.

The Excellent Wife and Mother

The inspired description of the excellent wife in Proverbs 31:10–31 should be studied by every family. All family members can benefit from such a study, as husbands learn what qualities to prize most highly in their mates, daughters learn what kind of women they should seek to become, and sons learn what traits to look for in a future spouse. Wives, of course, have described in this passage a wonderful composite of virtues worthy of imitation.

The woman depicted here is priceless (v. 10). Her husband has confidence in her judgment, knowing that "she does him good and not evil all the days of her life (v. 12). She is a bargain hunter (v. 14), a hard worker (vv. 15, 17–19), and a good money manager (v. 16). She might even work outside her home—without abandoning her children (v. 16). She is merciful to the needy (v. 20). Neither she nor her family is poorly or inappropriately attired (vv. 21–22). She brings credit and honor to her husband (v. 23). She is creatively industrious (v. 24), filled with moral and physical strength, and unafraid of the future (v. 25). She is self-controlled in her speech, using her words to instruct rather than to gossip (v. 26). Her main concern is her family, not wasting her time on selfish and frivolous pursuits (v. 27).

Is this not a truly liberated woman, freed from sin to be all that God intends her to be? Though some feminists today may sneer at this woman, "her children rise up and bless her; her husband also, and he praises her, saying: 'Many daughters have done nobly, but you excel them all'" (vv. 28–29). What mother would not like to have that said of her?

But to reap the harvest, you have to sow and tend the seed. God will not hold back His blessing from any mother who serves Him by cultivating her family according to His Word. Indeed, "A woman who fears the LORD, *she shall be praised. Give her the product of her hands,* and let her works praise her in the gates" (vv. 30–31). And when God commands that a mother be given the fruit of her labors, *who can keep her from her reward?*

May God give you who are mothers the grace to raise your children according to this beautiful standard. Not a single labor you exert in behalf of your little ones is unnoticed by your heavenly Father. Remember, Jesus said that what you do to His little ones, you are doing to Him (Matt. 18:5). Be willing, then, to work faithfully even in the obscurity of your homes.

I fully expect that faithful mothers will be among the most handsomely rewarded in heaven. Speaking of His disciples' rewards, Jesus taught, "But many who are first will be last; and the last, first" (Matt. 19:30). In the same way, many who have high-profile positions in the church will not be as lavishly rewarded in eternity as will many mothers. Why? Because God rewards us according to our faithfulness. That mother who cheerfully fulfills the arduous tasks involved in raising a family and guiding a household will be rewarded far more generously in eternity than the celebrity who does not use his time, contacts, and opportunities chiefly for the advancement of Christ's kingdom.

Moms, do not be consumed with your failures as a mother. Confess your sins, turn from them, and pray for grace to do your best. You have a perfect Advocate at the Father's right hand who will help you.

Discussion Questions

1. To what extent has America's materialistic culture affected your family's approach to the woman's traditional role as homemaker?
2. In your opinion, what is justifiable work outside the home and what is abandonment?
3. Contrast the Bible's teaching concerning needs with our society's definition of needs.
4. Discuss Titus 2:4–5 as it relates to us today.
5. How can the church better assist single mothers? Why should the church come to their aid?
6. What characteristics of "the worthy woman" most intrigue or impress you? Why?
7. Do you view the worthy woman of Proverbs 31 as a liberated woman? Why or why not?

❖ Chapter Twelve ❖

Encouragement for Parents Who Fail

The famous Christian author C. S. Lewis wrote:

> We all want progress. But progress means getting nearer to the place where you want to be. And if you have taken a wrong turning, then to go forward does not get you any nearer. If you are on the wrong road, progress means doing an about-turn and walking back to the right road; and in that case the man who turns back soonest is the most progressive. (*Mere Christianity*, 36)

We live in a day when people desperately want to feel good about themselves. Self-esteem is heralded as having an almost miracle-working power to raise individuals to new levels of success. If, as New Age teaching declares, we are "gods," then changing the image we have of ourselves as mere mortals is certainly important. But such teaching is arrogant fantasy to anyone who holds to a biblical worldview. All have sinned and fallen short of the glory of God (Rom. 3:23). The only cure for our desperate condition is to repent of our sin and to receive Jesus Christ as our Savior and Lord.

Facing Failure

Many parents who read this book will be convinced that they have failed in regard to their families. They may respond in one of two ways. They may attempt to minimize that failure by pointing to the failures of others around them. Or they may humble themselves and repent, as God would have them do. "He who conceals his transgressions will not prosper, but he who confesses and forsakes them will find compassion" (Prov. 28:13).

There is no benefit in deceiving ourselves and pretending that we have done no wrong if we have not kept our part in God's family covenant. But if we admit our failure to God, there is much that we can still do for our children's welfare, whatever their age. It is not too late to follow Lewis's admonition and turn back to the right way.

We are all failures. No one perfectly obeys even one of the commands of God—Christian or non-Christian. As parents, we are all in the same dilemma. We have all forsaken our duties to some degree. What can we say, then? Is there hope for any of us?

If God's plan of salvation were based on works, then we would have no grounds for hope concerning our own salvation, much less our children's. Salvation by works demands perfection. We must understand that God is perfect and heaven is a state of sinlessness. God cannot allow anyone into His eternal fellowship who is guilty of sin—any sin. To do so would compromise His nature and pollute heaven. And yet, we all "fall short of the glory of God" (Rom. 3:23). None of us measures up. "There is none righteous, not even one" (Rom. 3:10).

But the Bible also teaches that salvation is by grace, and that there is room for sinners to be redeemed from the consequences of their sins. Grace is God's love to the totally undeserving. "For by grace you have been saved through faith; and that not of yourselves, it is the gift of God; not as a result of works, that no one should boast" (Eph. 2:8–9). Salvation is a gift. It is not earned or merited. Through the death of the Son of God, the cost of sin has been paid. God "made Him who knew no sin to be sin on our behalf, that we might become the righteousness of God in Him" (2 Cor. 5:21). By accepting Christ, a believing sinner receives His perfect righteousness, is pronounced righteous, and is made a child of God (Rom. 3:24).

In the name of Christ, the forgiven sinner can embrace all the promises of God offered on the grounds of grace. The promises of God are applied to us by faith in Christ alone. And even that faith is a gift of His grace. Our imperfection, then, does not make God's promises void. The demand for perfection has been fully met by Christ in behalf of each one who trusts in Him. Praise God! Our hope is in His faithfulness, not ours. "God is faithful, through whom you were called into fellowship with His Son, Jesus Christ our Lord" (1 Cor. 1:9; see 2 Thess. 3:3).

Failing parents, then, can have hope that God's promises for their children have not been forever removed by their sinful irresponsibility. Do not misunderstand me. God has not changed. He has not lowered His divine standard but has fulfilled it for us through His perfectly obedient Son. Jesus alone could fulfill the standard of God's law and, by His own righteousness, merit an inheritance for all who trust in Him. In this way Christ has opened the door to all the promises of God for His people. That includes the promises given to parents concerning their children.

Doing Our Best While Resting in Grace

We saw in the opening chapters of this book that God's promises include the salvation of our children. These promises demand certain things of believing parents. And yet, we know that we cannot perfectly fulfill our duties. Does this mean that we are absolved from doing our best?

Absolutely not! God expects us to do our best. However, human effort *devoid of faith* is repugnant to Him because the worker stands before Him as a guilty sinner. Human effort, though, built upon a living faith in Christ is the delight of God. Although faith and works are not united as the *cause* of our salvation, they should be united as an *effect* of our salvation. God has even declared that all such efforts will be blessed with sure rewards! Paul announced, "My beloved brethren, be steadfast, immovable, always abounding in the work of the Lord, *knowing that your toil is not in vain in the Lord*" (1 Cor. 15:58).

Toil that is "in the Lord" is united to Christ by an active love and faith. Christ has redeemed us to be "a people for His own possession, zealous for good deeds" (Titus 2:14). He has commanded parents to give their best efforts, always looking to Jesus. As we strive to obey God in performing our parental duties, we do so totally resting in His grace, asking Him to superintend our best efforts at training and leading our children. When all is said and done, we trust His mercy to save our children, not our sin-laden attempts to obey Him. Every one of us should be willing to make the tough decisions, changing what needs to be changed in order to comply with His commands concerning our roles and duties in the home.

Turning Back Through Prayer

Parents who have not performed their duties ought to confess their sin to God and turn from it. *It is never too late with God*. Your children may be teenagers or even out of the home. Does that mean your children can't be saved? No, it doesn't—but it does demand that you use your greatest spiritual weapon as never before—*prayer*.

Like Paul, pray with the intensity of a woman giving birth until your children are saved (Gal. 4:19). Like Jacob, wrestle with God and do not let go until He answers (Gen. 32:24–30). When you have the opportunity, do what you can in the other three areas we have studied. You can offer your children biblical teaching as you would share the Word with another adult. You can even reprove them gently and with proper respect. You can live differently before them, showing them by your example that *your* life has changed. But these efforts will likely have little impact unless they are combined with prayer. Still, the God who delights in the prayers of the righteous (Prov. 15:8) will delight in answering you if you pray and do not give up. If you continually ask, seek, and knock—the Lord will give you the souls you seek (Matt. 7:7–8). Remember, He loves your children even more than you do.

Because God is sovereign, and we are insignificant creatures by comparison, we cannot command Him through our prayers. For His own good reasons, as well as for our good, His answers are not always immediate.

My family prayed for my brother Dave for thirteen years before he made a profession of faith. He had run away from home to pursue his dreams. For months at a time we did not know where he was. But my parents never gave up. They knew that the God to whom they were praying was always near their son.

I was visiting Dave in Florida when he told me that he wanted to talk. We sat down at a table, and I can still remember essentially what he said. "Ed, you once told me that I would never be happy until I turned to Christ. I didn't believe you, and I turned to everything else. What you said was right. Nothing else brings satisfaction and happiness. I want to receive Jesus today and become a child of God." To be honest, things have not all gone smoothly for Dave since his conversion. The old habits of sin have been very difficult for him to completely forsake. But we love him and pray for him, knowing that God is working in his life. Maybe there is someone like him in your life. Remember, every prayer that you utter is seed that you are sowing. Never give up on your loved ones—they need your prayers.

The blatant unbelief or immorality of your children might be breaking your heart even as you read this. *How will they ever turn to the Lord?* you might wonder. They oppose everything you stand for.

But does that bind the hands of God? Does it present Him with an insurmountable obstacle? Of course not. Our God created the world out of nothing. Your son's or daughter's spiritual blindness poses no great hurdle for Him.

Just how *big* is your God? Is He bigger than your children's sin and coldness? Our real struggle, you see, is with *our* lack of faith. With that in mind the apostles asked the Lord, "Increase our faith!" (Luke 17:5). That should be our request, too, if we are balking at the idea that the Lord can save our children. Say it *now* to God with your arms open wide: "Increase my faith!" If you have forsaken your parental duties, it will take great faith to pray for your children—but God can give it to you! Don't let your prior failures keep you from praying with faith now. You keep praying, and He will answer when it will bring Him the most glory.

Accepting Blame and Taking Hope

Are Christian parents to blame when their children do not come to faith in Christ? That's a tough question, but it is one that should be answered. It seems obvious to me that parents who have not faithfully kept their part of God's contract are partially to blame for the unbelief of their children. Our whole study demands that conclusion.

However, it is also true that blame rests on the unbelieving individual. A child's destiny turns with his or her own decision to follow Christ or to reject Him. If the child of believing parents rejects their faith, he or she is a covenant breaker (see Gen. 17:14; Isa. 24:5; Rom. 1:30). Every sinner will perish for his own iniquity, not for that of his parents. While the consequences of sin often are passed down from one generation to the next, no individual is condemned because of his parents' sin. God said, through Ezekiel: "The person who sins will die. The son will not bear the punishment for the father's iniquity, nor will the father bear the punishment for the son's iniquity; the righteousness of the righteous will be upon himself, and the wickedness of the wicked will be upon himself" (Ezek. 18:20). Likewise, Moses stated that "everyone shall be put to death for his own sin" (Deut. 24:16).

Therefore, every person must decide for himself whether to follow the Lord. That is equally true of children raised by disobedient parents and children raised by godly, obedient parents. The latter children are not saved because of their parents' obedience. Wonderful blessings come upon them through their parents, to be sure. But the children have to decide either to accept or to reject the Lord of their parents. The parents should not doubt God's promises to save their children. Nevertheless, the faith of the parents does not save the children. God saves the children. And it should be noted that He normally uses the faith and teaching of the parents to lead their children to Himself.

Thus, in no way are we advocating salvation by works. It is a question of means and ends. If God has designed to save children, what are the means that He employs to accomplish that end? I would insist that the normal channel used by the Lord is the child's parents.

No one accuses a missionary of advocating salvation by works when he says, quoting Paul: "How shall they believe in Him whom they have not heard? And how shall they hear without a preacher?" (Rom. 10:14). We all understand that God uses the means of a missionary's preaching to save the lost all over the world. It is the same in the home. How shall the children be saved without a parent's teaching, discipline, example, and prayer? These are the means normally ordained by God for the salvation of believers' children. God is the author of the means as well as the ends. He gives grace to parents to teach, discipline, model a Christian life, and pray. He deserves all of the glory, even while He makes use of Christian parents.

So, one reason for an individual's destruction is his own

unbelief. But another reason often is that his parents did not rightly raise him in the Lord. Therefore, I believe that before God, disobedient parents will be held accountable for forsaking their biblical duties toward their children. In some very real sense, the blood of our children will be on our hands if we do not keep our part of God's covenant with us. Are we not accomplices in their rebellion? Is it not we who are to teach them, discipline them, pray for them, and live as a godly example before them?

A person can be declared guilty of murder for shooting another human being. And a person who wrongly supplies a murderer with a gun and ammunition may also be charged in the crime, although to a lesser degree. Though we would never think of "pulling the trigger" to destroy our children, have we aided and abetted their misconduct by our disobedience?

If we have, each of us should repent of having wasted opportunities through the years. Having repented, however, we must not grovel in hopelessness. Christ died for the hopeless. There are no lost causes with an all-powerful God!

We should contact our children and humbly apologize for not raising them in a biblical manner. They may respect us for this or they may laugh in our faces and thank us for not raising them for Christ. We do not know when God will work. Whatever their response, we should pray for them as we have never prayed before. God will bless the prayers of the humble.

We also have the assurance that any sin truly repented of is forgiven by God. There is no sin that the repentant will be held responsible for. I have stated that parents are partially to blame for their children's spiritual rebellion. But they do not have to carry this blame with them before the judgment seat of Christ. Though it is a great sin, we have a God who is great in forgiveness. Let us thank Him for the fact that where sin abounds, grace does much more abound (Rom. 5:20): "If we confess our sins, He is faithful and righteous to forgive us our sins and to cleanse us from all unrighteousness" (1 John 1:9). Therefore all of us can freely confess our parental failures to God, asking Him to save our children, not because of our feeble efforts, but because of His matchless grace.

Discussion Questions

1. Discuss how and why all Christian parents are failures. What effect should this understanding have in our lives?
2. Why can't faith and works bring salvation to the sinner? How should faith and works unite in the believer's life?
3. Does God expect us to do our best? What if we don't—are the promises canceled? Explain.
4. What is the one great tool left for a believing parent who has failed to raise his children biblically? Discuss.
5. Discuss the promises of God concerning prayer (see chap. 3) and how they relate to our older unsaved children.
6. Are parents at fault for their children's unbelief? Discuss.
7. What has the Holy Spirit convicted you of in the area of parental failure? How should you respond?

❖ CHAPTER THIRTEEN ❖

"Children Are a Gift of the LORD"

When my parents left for Kenya, I was completing my first year in a college in Florida. They told me that while I was at school, I should work closely with a certain pastor in the Orlando area. They recommended that I go to him for counsel and relate to him as a spiritual mentor while they were abroad. My parents deeply loved and respected that man. I wasn't quite sure about him at first. He was rather old and eccentric. But I wanted to get my feet wet in all types of church work, and the Lord had always blessed me for submitting to my parents' desires; so I happily agreed.

I quickly became bonded to him and the people of his church. I was there every weekend helping in some way. He was a fascinating and mysterious man to me. Outwardly he seemed hard and abrupt, but underneath he was tender and compassionate. When asked, I agreed to work with the church for the summer, instead of getting a "regular" job to pay off my school debt.

His definition of church work and mine were quite different, I soon discovered. Operating both a church and a Christian school gave him the oversight of a good deal of property. And he had a thing about keeping everything just right. So he worked me hard. Picking oranges, removing deep-rooted palmetto "trees," scraping, painting, roofing, raking, mowing and edging lawns, clipping hedges, and scrubbing floors were all assigned duties. But I couldn't complain, because he was often sweating alongside me, dressed in his suit! Many times, when I was resting in the old trailer that was my home at the end of a brutal day of physical labor, I would hear a knock on the door. When I opened the door, all I would see was a bag full of ice cream, cakes, and other scrumptious delights. Then I would hear his car driving away.

My work wasn't all physical. There was the regular calling ministry in which I would accompany him from home to home like a shadow. Hour after hour he would drive in the sweltering summer sun of landlocked Orlando, never rolling down the windows of the car and refusing to use the air conditioner. Not exactly the type of ministry a young pastoral candidate longed for.

As an "old school" type, he had to break me in, I guess: you know, teach the younger generation a thing or two. I ended up working with him for three years. I had no job description and no contract. There were no promises. Once in a while he would give me money for gasoline plus a little extra. But I never went hungry, and he certainly didn't give me enough idle time to allow me to get bored. Frankly, I saw no strategy in his style of mentoring, and I didn't think I was getting a very good apprenticeship for pastoral work. I was wrong.

My parents knew that this man was God's gift to them and to me in a crucial time of our lives. As I look back, I think that my time spent with him was far more helpful in many ways than was my formal education. Those were days of real character testing and character building. He stressed and epitomized certain traits that are essential for a servant of God: Humility. Faithfulness. Love. Willingness to do anything that needs to be done. Doing all for Christ's glory and not expecting applause from man.

When he spoke of Christian service, the text he most often showed me was Luke 17:10: "So you too, when you do all the things which are commanded you, say, 'We are unworthy slaves; we have done only that which we ought to have done.'" He showed me and taught me that in fact "it is more blessed to give than to receive" (Acts 20:35). By the way, at the end of my college career, he raised all the money I needed to pay off my college debt!

I did not always see him as a gift from God. But he was. My life was changed in innumerable ways by his life and by what he put me through. I was truly blessed by God through him.

Good Gifts from God

Whatever form they come in, all of God's gifts are good. They are good because they come from the hand of an infinitely good God who knows just what we need.

Is your God a good God? Mine is. The Lord I serve does not gain pleasure by sending trouble into my life. Jeremiah said, "He does not afflict willingly, or grieve the sons of men" (Lam. 3:33). The trouble that does come upon His children is according to His perfect justice and is intended for His glory and their good (Rom. 8:28; Gen. 50:20). Trials and afflictions are allowed because they are well suited for helping us in our present sinful condition. Physical and material prosperity often do strange things to us, leading us away from God and towards self-dependence. We tend to put more trust in Him when we are suffering or shaken up, when our physical supports are threatened or removed.

The Lord never afflicts just for the sake of afflicting. Every trial God sends or temptation He allows in the lives of Christians is intended for our benefit. They never occur simply to annoy us or to make life miserable. That is why God also promises to provide a way of escape for us in every troubling situation (1 Cor. 10:13). He takes no pleasure in causing us discomfort. He just wants us to grow.

The Scriptures urge us to "give thanks to the LORD, *for He is good;* for His lovingkindness is everlasting" (Ps. 107:1). Either we believe that He is wholly good, or we regard Him as at least partially evil. Does your God have an evil streak that He often likes to indulge? Is He malevolent and evil by nature? As Christians we must reject such a notion and concur with Scripture that our God is a good and loving God.

If God is good, then the gifts He gives His people must also be good. Just think of some of the things that Scripture calls gifts from God. Jesus was the gift that God gave for the salvation of the world (John 3:16). Paul described the salvation of God as "His indescribable gift" (2 Cor. 9:15). The active indwelling of the Holy Spirit within the believer is termed "the gift of the Holy Spirit" (Acts 2:38). All that we receive from God in our salvation is a gift, whether the subject is grace (Eph. 3:7), justification (Rom. 3:24), or the imputed righteousness of Christ (Rom. 5:17). Is there anything unlovely in any of these wonderful gifts of God? Which of them would you choose to reject? They are all delightful and indispensable in our lives. A good God does not give gifts that are bad.

Children as God's Gifts

Do you realize that children are God's gifts to us, too? One of Solomon's psalms declares, "Behold, children are a gift of the LORD; the fruit of the womb is a reward. . . . How blessed is the man whose quiver is full of them" (Ps. 127:3, 5). If children of believers are called gifts from God, then they must have a good and necessary role to play in our lives.

What kind of gift would children be if we could not be certain that it was God's will to save them? How enriching to a couple's life is a child who grows up to rebel against his parents and to reject their God? What greater agony can occur in this world than that of seeing one's own child choose the foolish path of sin, court peril and despair all along the way, and inevitably die in the ugly grip of iniquity?

It has been my contention throughout this book that such a scenario does not have to occur in the families of Christians. God's promises and enabling grace are freely offered to all. The fact that so many reject these promises is not God's fault. No parent will stand in the day of judgment and accuse the Lord of ruining his life with monstrous children. One transforming gaze into the loving face of Christ will forever remove from our depraved hearts such a proud and self-deceived spirit. Our Jesus is infinite in His goodness.

When Esau saw his brother surrounded by a large number of children, he asked, "Who are these with you?" Jacob responded, "The children whom God has graciously given your servant" (Gen. 33:5; cf. Isa. 8:18). What a beautiful and accurate answer. Children are not only a gift. They are *gracious* gifts from God. We do not deserve them. Children are intended to produce all types of beneficial results in the lives of those to whom they come. And at every stage of development, that is exactly what they produce *for those who faithfully raise them in the way God has commanded.* Raising children for God is one of the most fruitful ways for parents to grow in Christ.

When we are faithfully overseeing our families, we don't have time to indulge in soul-destroying pursuits. Even the desire to walk in sin is reduced as we walk in the light with our children. God uses them as catalysts for our spiritual development. Instruction in God's Word, consistent Christian living, and prayer become greater parts of our lives as we lead our families biblically. These graces bring fullness and happiness to our lives. Those who forsake their parental roles unknowingly reject one of the greatest opportunities for spiritual growth they can possibly have. As instruments through which the Spirit causes parents to grow, children are indeed gracious gifts.

How Raising Children Helps Parents

My wife and I have three daughters and a son, all still living at home. The following are just a few benefits they have brought to us as we have prayerfully attempted to raise them for the Lord.

1. *We have realized that sin must be dealt with.* A child's sin cannot be overlooked, or it will grow worse and affect others. If we let one child get away with wrongdoing, we have established a precedent that every other child reminds us of and that brings bedlam into the household. For instance, we refuse to allow our children to hit each other. Regardless of how they may have been provoked or wronged, our children know that they have no right to physically hurt a brother or sister. If such violence is allowed, calamitous results can follow.

Debby and I have seen how this principle is true in our own spiritual lives, too. If we indulge one sin, it throws off our whole spiritual equilibrium. The Spirit of God is grieved when *any* sin is excused.

2. *We have discovered that prayer works.* Taking time to pray regularly and often makes the family run more smoothly. We teach our kids to pray whenever anything goes wrong. And they sometimes remind us to do the same with our parent-sized problems. Our private prayer life has grown considerably as a result of our praying with our children.

One prominent marriage counselor has said that in all his years of counseling, he never saw a single case of divorce arise between parents who prayed together every day. Prayer is beneficial for every aspect of life.

3. *We have learned that there is no time off from being a bib-lical parent.* Parenting demands constant attention. But instead of wearing us out, it has strengthened us. God created us all to be productive and industrious. Laziness is opposed to His original design and our new nature, which has been re-created in God's image. There is joy in *serving* Jesus. We drink from the water of life every time we do something in His name, and we are refreshed. We all fill our time by doing something—even if that something is nothing. And Debby and

I have not found anything more important or fulfilling than lovingly raising a family.

We have also learned through parenthood that there is no time off in our relationship with our heavenly Father, either. If we become spiritually lazy, we lose ground and feel as though we are cheating both ourselves and God because we are not living up to our potential in Christ. I don't mean to suggest that parents should never get time away from the kids. Parents need time alone with each other, when possible, perhaps even a day or two by themselves. But while you are with your family, there is no time off.

4. *Raising a family has taught us that it is better to give than to receive (Acts 20:35).* Parenting is all about giving. It is not far into the process of parenting that the character of parents is first severely tried. Will they live for themselves or for their child? Will they overcome the propensity to postpone their duties or give in to the delusion that a better time will come? Will they dedicate themselves to selflessly serving their child's best interests through biblical training? The parent who serves himself inevitably learns that he would have been better off doing his duty. It *is* better to give than to receive.

Every parent who reaps the reward of a godly family will confess that all the work and sacrifice was well worth it. Thus, raising a family prepares us for every other call to service in our lives. Having learned that it is better to give than to receive in our home, we are far better Christian servants. This is, indeed, a grace from God.

5. *We are often reminded that love is the most important element of a Christian home.* Love listens patiently. Love forgives and makes up. Love delights in another and lays aside its own agenda. Love cannot be destroyed; it never utterly fails. Love understands and gives the other person the benefit of the doubt. Love appreciates the uniqueness of individuals, not always trying to make people into clones. Love tries to put itself in the other's place.

It is in this way that the heavenly Father perfectly loves all His children. And this is how we are to love our children. Having by grace experienced this love for them, we find it much easier to love all of our brothers and sisters in Christ— which is Christ's greatest commandment (John 13:34).

6. *We've also learned that we must often say "I'm sorry" to our children.* We teach *them* to confess when *they* wrong others. We ought to confess when we have wronged them, as well. And we wrong them often! It is amazing how readily children forgive parents. To apologize to one's child is not such a bitter pill to swallow. Although pride keeps us from asking others' forgiveness, parents who develop humility toward their children are much more likely to admit their faults to others—especially to God. Everyone benefits when someone humbly confesses to wrongdoing. Repentance is thus another grace encouraged by the experience of raising children.

7. *Raising children teaches us that we need Jesus for everything.* A sincere parent soon learns that there must be a power at work in the home far greater than his or her own personal presence. That presence is Jesus. The Bible says that He is specially present wherever two or three persons are gathered in His name (Matt. 18:20). He is a permanent resident, then, in any Christian home led by parents intent on obeying His Word for His glory. Though we fail often and utterly, Jesus does amazing things in the homes of those who look to Him!

Our daughter Charity was having a very difficult time adjusting to her new Christian school environment when she entered high school. She found very few kids who were willing to accept her into their circles of friends. Some who did accept her weren't very strong spiritually. For a year we tried to help her through this struggle—and it was a struggle. The next summer she experienced a spiritual revival of her own after spending a couple of weeks with her godly grandmother. When she came home, she wept as she begged us to let her transfer to another Christian school so that she would not have to face some of her old friends. She was afraid of hurting them by no longer hanging out with them as much. She was also afraid of her own weakness and the possibility of being sucked back into a group of relationships that was less than edifying.

Debby and I sought God's wisdom. Then we told her that we could not agree with her changing schools. She couldn't run away from her relationships. We assured her that if she asked Jesus, He would help her through this problem. We knew that it was time for Charity to take her stand.

Jesus really did help her through it. Her last two years have been truly amazing. She discovered how she could live for Jesus and be a friend to everyone. Her fears that her old friends would leave her and "rag on her" didn't materialize. Jesus didn't let that happen. Instead, they respected her and continued to like her. And Charity was able to develop some new relationships that challenged and helped her spiritually.

My wife and I know that we cannot make a single change in our children's hearts. But Jesus can through the power of His Holy Spirit. Parents who look to Jesus in the home seek His guidance and power in all other areas of *their* lives. Charity's experience stimulated us toward a more conscious public association with Jesus, too. As parents we sometimes worry about what it might cost us if we clearly stand for Christ. Helping our daughter address her fears has helped us overcome our fears as well.

A Wealth of Children

Yes, children are a gracious gift of God. How unfortunate, then, is the tendency in our day to view them as a burden instead of a blessing. Are they a financial liability or an impediment in the path of self-fulfillment? Not if the Bible is your source of truth.

Describing the happy family, the psalmist wrote, "Your wife shall be like a fruitful vine, within your house, your children like olive plants around your table" (Ps. 128:3). Here is a picture of prosperity, not poverty. Children are an evidence of the blessing of God, not His curse. So instead of asking first of all, Can I afford to have children? we should ask, What does God say about the family, money, and contentment?

Paul promised his readers in Philippians 4:19, "My God shall supply all your needs according to His riches in glory in Christ Jesus." Do these words apply only to small families? I don't think so. Please don't misunderstand—I am not advocating irresponsibility. Much planning should go into building a family, primarily spiritual planning. Couples who bring children into the world enter into an agreement with God Himself concerning the little ones He gives them to raise in His name. Children, therefore, ought not to be simply the by-products of sexual union. Intense self-examination and prayer should go into the prospect of bearing children. And the question for every prospective parent is, Am I willing to raise this precious child as God has directed?

Every parent must reappraise his or her life with that question in mind. It is not an easy question in a society that measures happiness in terms of how much you possess—or how many material things you can give your children. Thousands of Christians today are depriving themselves, the church, and society of the gracious gifts of God because economics is the foremost consideration of their lives. Having bought into the materialistic worldview of their surrounding culture, they have forgotten that sound economics begins with trusting God, because "it is He who is giving you power to make wealth" (Deut. 8:18).

As Christians, we need to submit ourselves to the rule of Christ given to us in His Word. If we say that we love Him but do not obey His Word, we delude ourselves. But Jesus said, "He who has My commandments, and keeps them, he it is who loves Me; and he who loves Me shall be loved by My Father, and I will love him, and will disclose Myself to him" (John 14:21).

If we forsake the wisdom of the world in favor of the revelation of God, we will prosper in every way, along with our families. And we will soon discover what a blessing children can be! Notice how the psalmist's prayer for God's blessing in Psalm 144:11–15 envisions blessings regarding sons and daughters:

Rescue me, and deliver me out of the hand of aliens, whose mouth speaks deceit, and whose right hand is a right hand of falsehood. Let our sons in their youth be as grown-up plants, and our daughters as corner pillars fashioned as for a palace; let our garners be full, furnishing every kind of produce, and our flocks bring forth thousands and ten thousands in our fields; let our cattle bear, without mishap and without loss, let there be no outcry in our streets! How blessed are the people who are so situated; How blessed are the people whose God is the Lord!

May the Lord fill you with faith to believe His promises for you and your family. They are all yours through a living, personal faith in His Son, Jesus Christ, who said, "Let the children alone, and do not hinder them from coming to Me; for the kingdom of heaven belongs to such as these" (Matt. 19:14).

Discussion Questions

1. How does an understanding of the goodness of God assist us in our Christian lives?
2. In what ways have your children been gracious gifts of God to you?
3. Which of the seven benefits of raising children noted in this chapter most affected you? Why?
4. Is it important to try to change the way others think about having children and raising a family? Why? If so, how can this be done?
5. Discuss the role that financial considerations play in today's culture when couples make decisions about a family. Try to determine a balanced, biblical position for yourself.
6. Has this book lived up to your expectations? How has it or how has it not? Would you recommend it to others? Would you consider leading a class on it in your church?

❖ APPENDIX A ❖

Further Biblical Evidence

The following texts are relevant to our study, in that they speak of God's working within families. Most are positive promises of grace, though others are warnings of judgment. Many of the verses were omitted from the main body of this book for reasons of length and readability. I'll list them here in the order in which they appear in Scripture and include a few explanatory remarks on texts that might be unclear. This list is not exhaustive.

Old Testament Texts

Genesis 12:3
Leviticus 20:4–5
Leviticus 26:39
Deuteronomy 29:10-15
Joshua 24:14–15
1 Chronicles 13:14 (see 26:4–5)
Psalm 22:27-31

Psalm 25:12-14
Psalm 69:36
Psalm 102:28
Psalm 128:1-4
Proverbs 3:33
Proverbs 11:21
Proverbs 12:7
Isaiah 14:21–22
Isaiah 44:3
Isaiah 54:13 (see John 6:45)
Isaiah 61:9
Isaiah 65:23
Jeremiah 10:25
Jeremiah 31:1
Jeremiah 32:38–39
Ezekiel 16:20-21:

Moreover, you took your sons and daughters whom you had borne to Me, and you sacrificed them to idols to be devoured. Were your harlotries so small a matter? You slaughtered *My children*, and offered them up to idols by causing them to pass through the fire.

All the children whom the Israelites offered in pagan sacrifices God called "My children." In what way were they His children? They were children of promise, children with a special relationship with Him. They were His at least in virtue of the covenant that He had made with their parents.

Zechariah 14:17
Malachi 2:2–3

New Testament Texts

Matthew 23:29-36
Acts 3:25–26
1 Corinthians 7:13–14

And a woman who has an unbelieving husband, and he consents to live with her, let her not send her husband away. For the unbelieving husband is sanctified through his wife, and the unbelieving wife is sanctified through her believing husband; *for otherwise your children are unclean, but now they are holy.*

Charles Hodge explains these verses as follows:

The assertion of the apostle is, that the unbelieving husband or wife is sanctified in virtue of the marriage relation with a believer. . . . The Hebrew people were sanctified (i.e. consecrated), by being selected from other nations and devoted to the service of the true God. They were, therefore, constantly called holy. All who joined them, or who were intimately connected with them, became in the same sense, holy. Their children were holy; so were their wives. "If the first-fruits be holy, the lump is also holy; and if the root be holy, so are also the branches," Rom. 11:16. That is, if the parents be holy, so are also the children. Any child, the circumstances of whose birth secured it a place within the . . . commonwealth of Israel, was according to the constant usage of Scripture, said to be holy. *In none of these cases does the word express any subjective or inward change.* . . . When, therefore, it is said that the unbelieving husband is sanctified by the believing wife, and the unbelieving wife by the believing husband, *the meaning is, not that they are rendered inwardly holy,* . . . but that they were sanctified by their intimate union with a believer, just as the temple sanctified the gold connected with it; or the altar the gift laid upon it, Matt. 23:17, 19. . . . Thus, the pagan husband, in virtue of his union with a Christian wife, although he remained a pagan, was sanctified; he assumed a new relation; he was set apart to the service of God [sanctified], as the guardian of one of his chosen ones, and as the parent of children who, in virtue of their believing mother, were children of the covenant. (*An Exposition of the First Epistle to the Corinthians,* 115–16, emphasis added)

J. Oliver Buswell, Jr., also explains:

The clear teaching that a marriage is not to be broken on the grounds of difference of religious faith is followed by one of the great statements of the Scripture on the subject of the family covenant with God. "The unbelieving husband is made holy by the wife, and the unbelieving wife is made holy by the husband. Otherwise your children would be unclean, but as it is they are holy" (1 Cor. 7:14). The holiness here predicated is a holiness of a covenant relationship. Although Paul does not mention the word covenant, it is clear that he has in mind the principles implied in Genesis 17:7, "And I will establish my covenant between me and thee and thy seed after thee in their generations for an everlasting covenant, to be a God unto thee and to thy seed after thee." That fact that God is not only our God, but the God of our children, the God of our families, is emphatically taught throughout the Scripture, and should be regarded as a source of comfort to Christian parents in all ages and under all circumstances. God-fearing parents may, in confidence, claim the promise for their children, "I will be their God" (Gen. 17:8). It is on that basis that Paul declares that if one parent is a believer, the other members of the family are "sanctified" by the covenant relationship. (*A Systematic Theology of the Christian Religion,* 1:391)

Titus 1:6

If any man be above reproach, the husband of one wife, *having children who believe,* not accused of dissipation or rebellion.

If we cannot be sure about the salvation of our children, how can God make their salvation a requirement for an elder in the church? The fact that it is a qualification proves that parents can be sure about their children's eternal welfare. No one whose children (growing up under his Christian supervision) have rejected Christ is to be considered for the office of elder. If a candidate was saved later in life, when his children were older, he might stand as an exception. It is important to note, though, that an elder normally will be one who was saved early enough in his life to bring up his entire family in the faith.

We must also remember that someone may raise a child rightly but find that it is God's will to postpone communicating saving grace to that child until later in life. Such cases are exceptional. If there is a *trend* of spiritual rebellion in the home of an elder candidate (teaching or ruling elder) among children raised since his becoming a Christian, then he should be disqualified from consideration. God can use him elsewhere, but he is not best suited to be an elder.

1 Timothy 3:4–5

He *must* be one who manages his own household well, keeping his children under control with all dignity (but if a man does not know how *to manage his own household,* how will he take care of the church of God?

One who fails at effectively leading a few (the family) forfeits the right to lead many (the church). Andrew Murray comments:

Some may be inclined to doubt the truth of this statement. They have often heard, they know, of pious parents whose children have turned out ill. Is all the blame to be laid on the parents? We have no power to change evil nature; grace alone can do it. Is it not going too far to put the blame for unbelieving or unruly children on the parents and count such a fa-

152 ❖ FURTHER BIBLICAL EVIDENCE

ther unfit for holding office in the church or household of God because his own household is not what it should be? And yet this is just what the Holy Spirit does. He teaches Paul to connect unbelieving and unruly children with the failure of the home. (*How to Raise Your Children for Christ*, 265–66).

Though I would disagree with Murray's phrase "all the blame," the power of the text and his point should not be lost.

These last two references in the Pastoral Epistles should not be used to simply attack and dismiss church leaders who now hold office even though they have failed in the home. Such men could be reminded of these texts and lovingly asked to rethink their place of leadership. I would hope that the texts would mainly be used in the prayerful selection of future elders, so that unproven men are not advanced as leaders in Christ's church.

Most Common Objections

There are various reasons why doctrines fall out of favor with professing Christians. The very fact that the teaching presented in this book is *not* commonly believed today will raise some suspicion as to its veracity.

No one should accept a teaching unless it is founded clearly upon the Word of God and ratified to one's conscience by the inward teaching of the Holy Spirit (1 John 2:20, 27). I have attempted to stay within the teachings of the Word of God as I understand them. If I have rightly interpreted the texts in question, there should be evidence that other Christians writers down through the centuries have held the same view. I have quoted only a very small number of the respected authors who would concur with my position. I would like to have quoted more, but, again, reasons of length and readability have kept me from doing so.

Some readers will not agree with me and will no doubt raise objections. I would like to anticipate some of those objections and answer them briefly. First, let me restate my position clearly.

I believe that faithful parents can be sure that their children will be saved and go to heaven. This assurance is based on the promises of God to them and their families. There are conditions that parents are to meet, by God's grace, as the normal means to the salvation of their children. If parents abandon their responsibilities, then they have forsaken their agreement or covenant with God and have no reason to expect that the promises of God for their children's salvation will be fulfilled. Parents are to perform all their duties in a spirit of faith, looking to Jesus alone to make their efforts successful.

Children are not saved *because* of their parents. They are saved by grace through the redemption of Jesus Christ. Christian parents are simply the channel through which the message of this salvation is normally conveyed. They most likely will be the tools God uses to bring the salvation offered in His Son to their children. Though most children rightly raised will be saved and grow in grace early in their lives, some may not follow Christ until later. In such rare cases, the promised salvation is received, but not as quickly as anticipated.

Possible objections to this view can be divided into three basic types: experiential, theological, and biblical.

Experiential Objections

The most passionate objections arise from people who cite apparent exceptions to the above-stated position from the experience of Christian parents. Famous Christian leaders, godly adults, biblical characters, and simply good friends are noted as sometimes having wayward kids. How do we answer such alleged exceptions?

The problem is more emotional than actual, I believe. It involves *us* and *our* friends and beloved leaders. We hate to see them implicated in wrongdoing. We love them and don't want anyone pointing the finger at them and saying that they have done something wrong in their homes. That reluctance to find fault in others is commendable. We should be slow to judge parents whose children may come to faith later. As we have seen, God does sometimes postpone the conversion of rightly trained children. And we must remember that we all fail to some degree. The purpose of this book is to encourage you to look to Christ and to reflect on your own faithfulness—not to scrutinize others.

That being understood, unless we acknowledge that some parents' failure leads to their children's rebellion, we are forced to attribute failure instead to the promises of God. I do not believe that God breaks His promises or that He misleads us with His Word. I am not willing to forsake God's promises in deference to any human being, however much I might love and respect him or her.

Even if Debby and I fail in fulfilling our duties as parents and *our* children die in spiritual rebellion, would that disprove this book? I do not think so. The promises of God stand. It would prove only that *we* failed and took our eyes off Jesus and His promises.

It is possible to be mightily used by the Lord in one sphere and to fail in another. Examples in the Bible include successful leaders who were horribly deficient parents. Visible success or outward involvement in the life of the church do not guarantee that all is well in one's heart or one's home. One couple I know of, who complained about their wayward child, argued that they always had the child in church whenever the door was open. What went wrong? They mistook their mechanical obedience for prayerful, effective ministry to their children's hearts by the power of the Holy Spirit.

Promises are promises, and it is dangerous to argue against the promises of God. We are responsible for our lives as individuals in every sphere—including parenthood. If we fail as parents, we should not be surprised to reap the consequences. Though God often overrules our failures, He does not always undo the consequences of parental disobedience. But He does always deliver on His promises to faithful parents.

At stake is God's testimony or glory. What type of God would we have if He did *not* keep His promises, or if He did *not* answer prayer that is based on His Word?

Theological Objections

While various theological arguments arise over this subject, none of them is insurmountable. The chief theological challenge comes from those who say that my whole position savors of a mixture of grace and works. I have been sensitive to this concern throughout the writing of this book, and I affirm unequivocally that every person's salvation is *totally* of grace. There is *no* place for human merit or works as a cause of salvation. Jesus is the cause.

At the same time, God uses various means to apply the salvation procured by Christ. The normal means for an unsaved adult is the Christian witness of a minister or layperson. "How shall they believe in Him whom they have not heard?" Paul asked in Romans 10:14. Is this salvation by grace plus works? Of course not. God uses believers as messengers, but He alone does the saving. Likewise, the normal means by which a child of believers comes to faith in Christ is the faithful instruction, discipline, example, and prayers of his or her parents. In neither case are works a cause of salvation.

The difference between those two examples is that we cannot be sure of the response of an adult to whom we are witnessing. There is no promise from God that any or all to whom we witness will be converted, although some will likely be saved. However, as we have seen, there are promises concerning the salvation of a believer's child. The criticism that my position mixes grace and works in regard to the salvation of children is simply untrue.

Another theological problem sometimes mentioned is that this teaching seems to contradict the doctrine of election (i.e., that God has from all eternity chosen some to everlasting life). Some think that if God has given the promise of salvation to believing parents concerning their children, then all such children must be elect. However, they argue, not all children of believers become saved and go to heaven, and so it is evident that not all of them *are* elect.

I have never said that all the children of believers are elect or that they all shall be saved. Just as God offers the promise of salvation to all who believe, so He offers to parents the assurance that their children will believe and be saved *if* the parents embrace God's promises and raise their kids in His way. The promise of God to parents is based on the grace that He gives them to do their biblical duties in the home. Only the parents of elect children will be given the faith to believe the promises of salvation offered by God for their children. And only such parents will be graciously enabled to perform their part of the covenant God made with them for their families. God does not work against Himself.

Involved in this whole issue is the difficulty of reconciling the sovereignty of God with the responsibility of human beings. But the Scriptures clearly teach both doctrines, even in the same passage (see, for example, Acts 2:22–23; 4:27–28; Phil. 2:12–13; 2 Tim. 2:19)! So, whether or not we can fully understand how God's sovereignty and human responsibility interrelate, we must accept both doctrines. God has ordained from eternity whatever comes to pass, but He has done so in such a way that He is not the author of sin. Neither does He predestine in such a way that our individual responsibility is removed or lessened. That is the teaching of Scripture, and it takes faith to receive it as such.

Another theological obstacle to some is that our position seems to be based solely on covenant theology as opposed to dispensational theology. That objection is inaccurate. We must guard against overstating the differences between these two theological positions. Some dispensationalists teach that covenant theology denies the varied manner in which God worked throughout biblical history. But covenant theologians do note significant differences in the progressive unfolding of redemption, and some even use the word *dispensation* to signify these differences (see Charles Hodge's *Systematic Theology* [abridged], 344–50). There are also many dispensational theologians today who admit the great importance of the Old Testament and New Testament covenants, integrating them into their theological positions. Thus, both groups use the words *dispensation* and *covenant*.

The issue with which this book is concerned is the promise of salvation. Both groups affirm that believers can be saved only by grace through faith. And both groups believe that God's promises relate to us today. That being the case, whatever other differences might divide these two theological positions (and they have been narrowing), our subject should not be a point of contention between them. We have shown how believers in both Testaments had promises of salvation extended to their children. On *that* issue there need be no debate. It would serve no purpose, then, to tag me with a theological label in order to dismiss my position. It must be tested by the Scriptures.

Biblical Objections

I have encountered several passages that on the surface seem to oppose the teaching that God offers parents the promise of salvation for their children. Before looking at these, it is good to remember a general rule of Bible interpretation: less clear texts are to be interpreted in the light of clearer texts. That is, obscure texts give way to clearer texts when there is a seeming inconsistency between them. Those who believe in the inerrancy of Scripture affirm that there are no insurmountable inconsistencies in the Bible. This must be so if the God of truth is its Author. And so, as we examine the following texts, bear in mind the vast number of biblical texts we have already seen, many of which clearly reveal God's promises to parents for their children.

Ezekiel 18

The sinful children of Israel were trying to explain their awful condition as being simply the consequence of their fathers' rebellion. In this way, they were justifying their own wickedness and rebellion. The common saying was, "The fathers eat the sour grapes, but the children's teeth are set on edge" (v. 2). It was a clever maneuver by which sin was justified rather than honestly dealt with.

In response, Ezekiel delivered a wonderful message on the justice of God in His relationship with individuals. He gave hypothetical situations (using "if's" throughout) that covered all possible cases. The sons of good men will be judged if they do not follow their fathers' path. And good sons will be blessed if they forsake their fathers' wickedness.

The point of this passage is *not* to disprove the promises of God to believing parents. It is, rather, to illustrate clearly that God is just and that no one will be condemned for the sins of another, as summarized in verse 4: "Behold, all souls are Mine; the soul of the father as well as the soul of the son is Mine. The soul who sins will die." It is important not to force such an illustration or parable into proving or disproving something it does not even deal with.

Matthew 10:21, 35–37

> And brother will deliver up brother to death, and a father his child; and children will rise up against parents, and cause them to be put to death. . . . Do not think that I came to bring peace on the earth; I did not come to bring peace, but a sword. For I came to set a man against his father, and a daughter against her mother, and a daughter-in-law against her mother-in-law; and a man's enemies will be the members of his household. (See Luke 12:49–53; Mic. 7:1–2, 6.)

Jesus did not want His disciples to think that following Him would be easy. Some of them mistakenly thought that He was going to bring in the physical kingdom of God at that time (see Luke 19:11), and they were even ready to argue about who would have the most eminent place in that kingdom (Luke 9:46; 22:24). Knowing that His disciples' expectations were wrong, Jesus wanted to prepare them for the tremendous trials that were before them.

It is also important for us to keep in mind that the instruction given in Matthew 10 was specifically designed for the

Twelve, whom Jesus sent out on a specific mission. The passage has many parallels and applications for our lives, too, but it was not primarily spoken to us. Its scope was limited by Jesus saying, "Do not go in the way of the Gentiles, and do not enter any city of the Samaritans; but rather go to the lost sheep of the house of Israel" (vv. 5–6). No one suggests that this restriction is binding on us today. A quick reading of the passage shows several other points that were unique to the apostles' day and ministry.

In light of this background, consider the verses that I have quoted. Verse 21 states a hard fact to grown men. Some of their fathers will oppose them. Moreover, some of the young believers converted through their ministry will be opposed by their fathers, and some of the older converts will be opposed by their children. None of these statements contradict the covenant promises. Jesus simply did not want the disciples to think that the world would fall down before them or accept them with open arms.

Verses 34–39 were also intended to clear up the disciples' misperceptions. Jesus began, "Do not think . . ." because He knew what they were thinking—that He had come to bring peace alone. He certainly came to bring peace, as the angels declared to the shepherds (Luke 2:14), but that was in the spiritual realm. The physical realm was quite a different story— as Herod proved by slaughtering the infants, and as Simeon had earlier prophesied (Luke 2:34–35). The disciples had to learn that Jesus would not inaugurate world peace at that time.

The statements made in verses 34–36 must be understood in this context. Jesus is not saying that there is no longer an agreement between God and believing parents. What He is saying is that a person's love for God must be greater than any other human bond (v. 37). In this way, family relationships can serve as a test of a person's greatest love. Instead of overturning God's promise to parents concerning their children, this text warns the disciples of the inevitable struggles that many followers of Christ face, struggles that even involve family members.

Romans 9:10–23

The case of Isaac and Rebekah could be seen as a difficulty for my position. Isaac was a son of promise (v. 8) who had the covenant of God extended to him (Gen. 26:3–5). Nevertheless, his two sons, born of the same mother, had different relationships with God. Paul's argument in this text is that physical descent from Abraham does not secure a portion in the promised inheritance (v. 7). A person is saved because he has been chosen by God (v. 11), not for *any* human reason. Those who receive Christ are spiritually reborn "not of blood, nor of the will of the flesh, nor of the will of man, but of God" (John 1:13).

The line of Messiah could come through only one of Isaac's descendants. Why was Jacob chosen for that honor instead of Esau? We can respond only as Jesus did in Matthew 11:26: "Thus it was well-pleasing in [God's] sight."

The use of the words "loved" and "hated" in reference to Jacob and Esau (Rom. 9:13) has sometimes been used to portray the Lord as a cold and hard being. Charles Hodge's notes on these words are worth repeating, as they preserve a more exalted and biblical understanding of God's nature:

> The meaning, therefore, is that God preferred one to the other, or chose one instead of the other. As this is the idea meant to be expressed, it is evident that in this case the word *hate* means *to love less, to regard and treat with less favor.* Thus in Gen. 29:33, Leah says, she was hated by her husband; while in a preceding verse, the same idea is expressed by saying, "Jacob loved Rachel more than Leah;" Also see Matt. 6:24; Luke 14:26; "If a man come to me and hate not his father and mother, etc." John 12:25. (*Commentary on the Epistle to the Romans,* 312)

God is sovereign in dispensing His blessings; but He also is a covenant-keeping God. The promises that He has made to us can be relied on. God does not oppose Himself. His divine election works hand-in-hand with His enabling parents to claim and to keep His agreement concerning their children. If He has chosen your children, He will also save them. And the means most often used in saving children is their conscientious and biblical training by their parents. None of us knows who the elect are before they are saved. Do not stumble over that uncertainty. Do your part and you can be sure that the Lord will do His part.

These are the major objections to my position. More may surface, but I do not foresee any serious threats to God's family promises. The Bible is internally consistent, and no one text can truly subvert another. Great effort and study may be necessary to answer all objections, but the truth of God will stand.

Negative and Positive Promises of God

Important to our subject is the difference between a negative promise of God and a positive promise of God. A negative promise may be one of judgment or destruction of a person or group. Positive promises are His pledges of blessing, life, and the like.

God will sometimes alter a negative promise through His mercy and grace, replacing it with a positive blessing. He saves death-deserving sinners by giving them spiritual life. Why does He do this? It is because of His infinite love. God will always replace His sentence of judgment on a person or people when they truly repent of sin and turn to Him. Although He said, through Jonah, that He would destroy Nineveh, the Lord did not send His judgment after the citizens repented. Instead He replaced a negative promise with a positive blessing.

God often revealed a desire to relent through His prophets:

At one moment I might speak concerning a nation or concerning a kingdom to uproot, to pull down, or to destroy it; if that nation against which I have spoken turns from its evil, I will relent concerning the calamity I planned to bring on it. (Jer. 18:7–8; see also Jer. 26:3; 36:3; Ezek. 18:21–23; 33:11, 14–15; Joel 2:12–14)

But will God ever replace a positive promise that is embraced and sincerely followed with a negative response? No. He will never promise good and then do evil in return. He will not promise salvation to an individual and then send the justified believer to hell. Neither will he send the children of covenant-keeping parents to hell. He might, however, because of His divine wisdom, choose to postpone giving the offspring saving grace until later in life.

How could postponing a person's salvation possibly be helpful? Sometimes the trials that we are allowed to endure make us wiser and humbler than we would otherwise have been. A child of faithful parents who is left to wander in sin for a while may become the means by which many come to Christ. Someone who has gone through a particular trial can empathize with struggling sinners and, perhaps, more powerfully address their specific needs. He can at least assure them from experience that Jesus has the power to help them. What believing parent would accuse God of unfaithfulness or wrongdoing if his child was allowed to wander in sin so that many others would, through him, come to know Christ? As the heaven is higher than the earth, so are God's ways higher than our ways. God is good and faithful and loving.

Though it is an almost intolerable burden to see a child of faithful parents turn away, we should not hastily conclude that there is no covenant at work here. Neither should we conclude that God is anything but good. Parents who undergo such a manifestation of providence ought to be embraced, loved, and comforted with God's promises instead of being blamed. They do not need to feel guilty. They need to be loved and encouraged to persevere in their faith, believing in the promises of God to the end. "Let us hold fast the confession of our hope without wavering, for He who promised is faithful" (Heb. 10:23).

❖ Appendix D ❖

The Salvation of Children Dying in Infancy

It is commonly affirmed among evangelicals that children who die before they reach an age of accountability (whatever that might be) will go to heaven. I concur with that belief, although I admit that the Scripture is not explicitly clear in this regard. David's assurance concerning his dead infant son is instructive (2 Sam. 12:15–24). The son was born of an illegitimate union, involving murder, and died before officially becoming a covenant child (on the eighth day by circumcision). And yet David seems to have been hopeful of seeing the child in heaven, which may have been the basis for the comfort he offered Bathsheba as well. If David's child was saved, one might argue, whose would be lost? The following statements of two well-known Christian authors express this same idea:

John Newton (1725–1807)

I think it is at least highly probable, that when our Lord says, "Suffer little children to come unto me, and forbid them not, for of such is the kingdom of heaven," (Matt. 19:14), he does not only intimate the necessity of our becoming like little children in simplicity, as a qualification without which . . . we cannot enter his kingdom, but informs us of a fact, that the number of infants who are effectually redeemed to God by his blood, so greatly exceeds the aggregate of adult believers, that, comparatively speaking, the kingdom may be said to consist of little children. The apostle speaks of them as not having "sinned after the similitude of Adam's transgression," Rom. 5:14, that is, with the consent of their understanding and will. And when he says, "We must all appear before the judgment seat of Christ," he adds, "that every man may give an account of what he has done in the body, whether it be good or bad," 2 Cor. 5:10. But children who die in their infancy have not done anything in the body, either good or bad. It is true they are by nature evil, and must, if saved, be the subjects of a supernatural change. And though we cannot conceive how this change is to be wrought, yet I suppose few are so rash as to imagine it impossible that any infants can be saved. The same power that produces this change in some, can produce it in all; and therefore I am willing to believe, till the Scripture forbids me, that infants, of all nations and kindred, without exception, who die before they are capable of sinning after the similitude of Adam's transgression, who have done nothing in the body of which they can give an account, are included in the election of grace. They are born for a better world than this; they just enter this state of tribulation; they quickly pass through it. . . . Should I be asked to draw the line, to assign the age at which children begin to be accountable for actual sin, it would give me no pain to confess my ignorance. (*The Works of John Newton*, 719)

Charles Hodge (1797–1878)

Charles Hodge supported his belief that all infants dying in their infancy are saved with the following statement:

> One of the Scripture's teachings on the subject of salvation, according to the common doctrine of evangelical Protestants, is that all who die in infancy are saved. This is inferred from . . . Romans 5:18–19. We have no right to put any limit on these general terms, except what the Bible itself places upon them. The Scriptures nowhere exclude any class of infants, baptized or unbaptized, born in Christian or in heathen lands, of believing or unbelieving parents, from the benefits of the redemption of Christ. All the descendants of Adam, except those of whom it is expressly revealed that they cannot inherit the kingdom of God, are saved. This appears to be the clear meaning of the apostle, and therefore he does not hesitate to say where sin abounded, grace has much more abounded; that the benefits of redemption far exceed the evils of the fall. (*Systematic Theology* [abridged], 37–38)

Works Consulted and Cited

Bonk, Jonathan. *Missions and Money*. Maryknoll, N.Y.: Orbis Books, 1991.

Bridges, Charles. *A Commentary on Proverbs*. Edinburgh: Banner of Truth, 1974.

Buswell, J. Oliver. *A Systematic Theology of the Christian Religion*. Grand Rapids: Zondervan, 1962.

Calvin, John. *Calvin's Commentaries*. Translated by John King. 22 vols. Grand Rapids: Baker, 1984.

Edwards, Jonathan. *Complete Works of Jonathan Edwards*. 2 vols. Edinburgh: Banner of Truth, 1974.

Flavel, John. *The Works of John Flavel*. 6 vols. Edinburgh: Banner of Truth, 1982.

Henry, Matthew. *Commentary on the Whole Bible*. 6 vols. Old Tappan, N.J.: Revell, n.d.

Hodge, A. A. *Evangelical Theology*. Edinburgh: Banner of Truth, 1976.

Hodge, Charles. *Commentary on the Epistle to the Romans*. Grand Rapids: Eerdmans, 1972.

_____. *An Exposition of the First Epistle to the Corinthians.* Grand Rapids: Eerdmans, n.d.

_____. *Princeton Sermons.* Edinburgh: Banner of Truth, 1979.

_____. *Systematic Theology.* 3 vols. Grand Rapids: Eerdmans, 1960.

_____. *Systematic Theology.* Abridged by Edward N. Gross. Grand Rapids: Baker, 1988.

Hoeksema, Herman. *Reformed Dogmatics.* Grand Rapids: Reformed Free Publishing Association, 1966.

Hopkins, Ezekiel. *The Works of Ezekiel Hopkins.* 3 vols. Philadelphia: Leighton, 1874.

Lawson, George. *Proverbs.* Grand Rapids: Kregel, 1980.

Lewis, C. S. *Mere Christianity.* New York: Manhattan, 1978.

Murray, Andrew. *How to Raise Your Children for Christ.* Minneapolis: Bethany Fellowship, 1975.

Newton, John. *The Works of John Newton.* London: Henry G. Bohn, 1871.

Poole, Matthew. *A Commentary on the Holy Bible.* 3 vols. Edinburgh: Banner of Truth, 1963.

Scott, Thomas. *The Holy Bible with Explanatory Notes, Practical Observations and Copious Marginal References.* 3 vols. New York: W. E. Dean Printer & Publisher, 1846.

Spurgeon, Charles H. *The Treasury of David.* 7 vols. Grand Rapids: Guardian Press, 1976.

20 Centuries of Great Preaching. 13 vols. Waco, Tex.: Word, 1971.

Ursinus, Zacharias. *Commentary on the Heidelberg Catechism.* 1852. Reprint. Phillipsburg, N.J.: Presbyterian and Reformed, 1988.

Watson, Thomas. *A Body of Divinity.* Grand Rapids: Sovereign Grace, n.d.

Witherspoon, John. *The Works of John Witherspoon.* 3 vols. Philadelphia: William W. Woodward, 1800.

Scripture Index